The Sounds of Children

FREDERICK WILLIAMS
University of Southern California

ROBERT HOPPER
University of Texas at Austin

DIANA S. NATALICIO
University of Texas at El Paso

Prentice-Hall, Inc., Englewood Cliffs, New Jersey 07632

Library of Congress Cataloging in Publication Data

Williams, Frederick, (date)
    The sounds of children.

    Bibliography: p.
    Includes index.
        1. Language arts (Elementary)—United States.
2. English language—Dialects—United States.
3. Children—Language.   I. Hopper, Robert, joint
author.   II. Natalicio, Diana S., joint author.
LB1576.W4884   372.6   76-41823
ISBN 0-13-823062-5

To . . . All of the children of the world,
        Black and yellow, red and white,
        They are precious in His sight . . .

        (traditional children's song)

Printed in the United States of America.

10   9   8   7   6   5   4   3   2   1

Prentice-Hall International, Inc., *London*
Prentice-Hall of Australia Pty. Limited, *Sydney*
Prentice-Hall of Canada, Ltd., *Toronto*
Prentice-Hall of India Private Limited, *New Delhi*
Prentice-Hall of Japan, Inc., *Tokyo*
Prentice-Hall of Southeast Asia Pte. Ltd., *Singapore*
Whitehall Books Limited, Wellington, *New Zealand*

Contents

Preface

Our aim is to provide you with a "sense" of children's language. Whether you are a speech or language student, a teacher, a parent, or just someone who cares about children, *The Sounds of Children* provides a picture of the current view of language, how it is considered in child development, how children differ, and how we tend to develop attitudes about children's language.

We have tried to overcome two major obstacles in preparing *The Sounds of Children*. First, we have avoided technical terminology as much as possible. Where it has been necessary, we have attempted to give you concise, plain-language definitions. Second, we have used samples of children's speech as *best* examples of points that we wished to illustrate. These samples appear in the text and on the accompanying records. Although the records and text are designed for independent use, we believe that together they provide examples second only to real-life experience.

Our only advice is that in reading and listening to the children in this book you try to enjoy yourself as much as they did, doing the talking.

Frederick Williams
Robert Hopper
Diana Natalicio

About the Recordings...

Every example of children's speech in this text is also on the accompanying recordings and in the same order. The points made in most text examples usually can be understood without hearing the recording, and we have included comments and transitions of the records so you may listen to them without the book.* Ultimately, however, the combined experiences should give you a firsthand sense of many aspects of children's speech that we consider important.

Most of the recording was prepared by Robert Hopper, and his voice is in the transition sections. However, all authors worked closely in determining the selections and final editing. Thanks are due to Alfred G. Smith for making recording equipment available and to Kathleen Jamieson, Donald Ecroyd, Ethel Glenn, Robert Ware, and Robert Cate for providing samples. In addition to the authors, fieldworkers included Sally Baumgardner, Cindy Fernandez, Grace Flores, Elise Keeney, David Lopez, and Donna Cornell.

*Smaller type in text examples indicates conversation not included in recording.

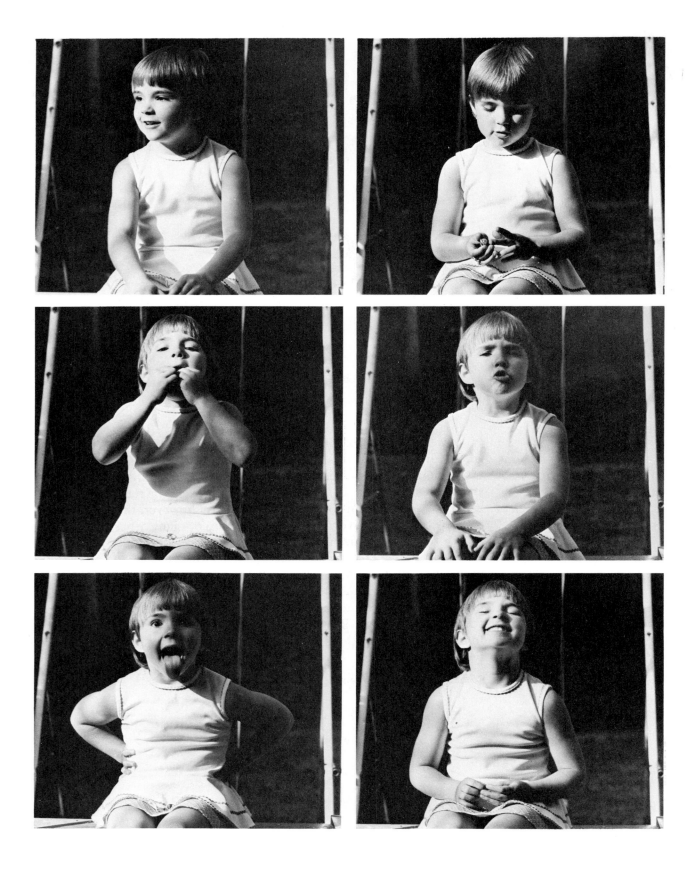

The New View of Language

1

OK now . . .

We got some hot dogs . . . for dinner.

We got some hot dogs.

Hot dogs . . . Wieners!

We got some HOT DOGS

. . .

and WIENERS!

We got some HOT DOGS . . .

. . . WIENERS!

We got some w_i_e_n_e_r_s . . .

. . . We got some wieners in the sky.

. . . We got some wieners in the rock.

W_I_E_N_E_R_S . . . HA!

Many of the sounds of children are happy sounds. (Who else could be so happy with hot dogs for dinner?) If you are like most people, children's speech is such an everyday experience that you probably have never thought of it as anything very complicated. Yet many contemporary scientists agree that the development of speech in children, especially as it is tied to thinking, is probably one of the most challenging topics in the human sciences.

At the outset it will be helpful to clarify at least generally what is meant by *speech* and *language*. We usually consider *speech* to be those vocal behaviors we can observe directly. We assume that there is some underlying knowledge in the minds of speaker and listener that relates those behaviors to meanings. This underlying knowledge of relations between sounds and meanings we usually call *language*, and in this sense we are using the term abstractly. We can, of course, be more concrete and refer to the French language or the Japanese language. Then we are considering what essentially are variations in how sets of sounds are related to sets of meanings. Although, these are simplified definitions they also are practical ones for the time being.

In the last decade we have witnessed a revolution in the study of the processes by which children learn language. Most of this revolution has yet to reach the general public, and only parts of it have filtered through to such persons as teachers who do practical work with children. The crux of the matter is that we now recognize more than ever that child language is a *unique* type of human behavior. For many years it was assumed that children acquired language simply because infants were good learners and because parents provided many learning reinforcements for speech. In the new view, however, it has been recognized that children's acquisition of language reflects the remarkable uniqueness of the human brain and its power to acquire a symbol system. There is nothing we know of in our existence— animal or machine, including the wildest dreams of computer designers—that can come to wield in such a short time the symbol power of a child learning to talk.

Child language is a far broader topic than it might seem at first. For one thing, language is the way society "gets into" a child. *A* language (English, Chinese, and so forth) carries with it many of the priorities of a society, its values, and attitudes. (Can you recall reading how Eskimos have many extra words for types of snow or Arabs for desert conditions?) Even the dialects or styles of a language carry with them such priorities. (We cannot adequately translate into so-called "standard" English the nuances of such Black English terms as "jive," "sound," "the man," and so on.) Language plays a key role in the acculturation process. The language styles of a family will determine the language and cognitive styles of the next generation of that family as they are manifested in the children. Language is a means by which one generation transmits its culture to another.

Can the language learning process be facilitated? Probably so, if we understand more of how children learn language. The admonition largely is to provide them with rich and varied linguistic experiences—not just talking *to* children but *with* them. The tendency to overcorrect a child may inhibit speech. What *is* most important is to give him or her a sense of language as communication. What will language do *for* and *to* that child?

Language also plays a role in preparing the child to shift from the family to wider social contacts and eventually to the schoolroom. The extent to which language develops effectively carries a variety of consequences for the child's success in school. Language is the most fundamental of subjects; it is the one through which all others are made intelligible.

We do have some problems with language in our society. Some children must learn two languages or dialects to communicate in the home as well as outside the home or in school. Some dialects seem to "mark" a child socially with certain expected patterns of behavior.

Until the last decade, explanations of child language development were usually relegated to brief textbook sections or at most, a chapter. Those of us who were students 20 years ago learned that children acquired language mainly as a process of experience and reward. That is, a child might hear "ball" while seeing one and learn the association between word and thing. Or a child would imitate the word and be rewarded with a smile (or getting the ball). This approach more or less viewed language development as a rather complex version of how we teach our dog to shake hands or a parrot to "talk." Current thinking on child language development is much different.

Toward the New View

As we wrote in the Preface, our aim is to give you a "sense" of children's language. To do this it will be useful to introduce a few theoretical issues that we group under the following headings: linguistic, psychological, and socio-logical aspects of child language study. A knowledge of these issues will help you to understand why certain approaches are taken in current research in child language. Even more practically, such knowledge will help clarify why certain assumptions about instructional practices have come into vogue. Here are a few, overall, introductory comments:

1. In the early 1960s, a new approach to linguistic theory prompted a major revolution in the types of questions asked about child language development. Main among these questions was: What exactly is it that a child learns when he learns language? Broadly, the answer was that a child learns a system of rules that relate sounds to meanings. The new linguistic theory provided ideas as to the nature of these rules.

2. The new linguistic theory drew a sharp line between generalizations about linguistic rules (properly considered within the domain of linguistics) and generalizations about how people *behave* with such rules (a topic relegated to psychologists). Consequently, new psychological theories emerged to describe child language development. At first, these theories were closely identified with linguistic concepts as researchers tried to characterize the "psychological reality" of linguistic rules. Toward the end of the 1960s it became increasingly clear that the "fit" between linguistic

theory and generalizations about child language was not as promising as
first thought. Psychological studies of child language in the mid-1970s
still reflect linguistic generalizations, but at more of a distance than in
the 1960s. Further, there now is more of a tendency to adapt linguistic
concepts to better serve psychological theories than heretofore was done.

3. Particularly because of the impetus given language research during
the War on Poverty years in the United States, a concern with language
differences among children emerged. Dialects and other aspects of
language variation had not been of central interest in linguistic theory, nor
in the associated psychological approaches. However, the decade of the
1960s also was marked with significant strides in the study of language
differences in children or, more abstractly, of the relations of language to
social factors.

Let us now consider these aspects in a bit more detail.

LINGUISTIC THEORY

The "new" linguistic theory was developed chiefly from the works of
Noam Chomsky in the late 1950s and early 1960s—a theory called *generative*
or *transformational grammar.* This theory stresses language as the *knowledge*
a person must have to relate sounds and meanings, and that knowledge can
presumably be described in terms of different types of rules.

A fundamental assumption in Chomsky's theorizing is that the ability
to develop language is part of our human genetic endowment. Just as we
have evolved into two-legged, walking creatures, we have developed a brain
that allows us to learn a highly complex set of relations between sounds and
meanings—a system called language. We assume that at the heart of this
system are sets of rules that interrelate all the details of language structure
with the meanings the speakers of a language share.

What is a linguistic rule? Psychologically speaking, we don't exactly
know, but we can easily see evidence of them in children's speech. See
if you can detect the rules in the following conversation with a seven-year-
old:

> *We are looking at a picture of an odd animal; the interviewer says:*
> This is a "glutch." In this picture there are two of them.
>> Child: Glutch
>> There are two of them, right?
>> Two glutches.

This is a man who knows how to "rick." He is ricking. He did the same thing yesterday. What did he do yesterday? Yesterday, he . . .

Ricked.

Good. With this picture you could say, "The ball was hit by the boy." What other way could you say it?

The ball was hit by the bat.

You could say the ball was hit by the bat. Is there any way you could say it that starts with "The boy?"

. . . Silence.

Could you say that "The boy . . . hit the ball?"

Uh huh.

Would that mean the same thing?

Uh huh.

Okay. This one you could say, "The bone was found by Snoopy." What other way could you say it?

The bone was found by Charlie.

But Charlie isn't there.

Uh . . . he unburied the bone.

Okay. How could you say it starting with "Snoopy . . . ?

Found . . . ?

Okay. Say the whole sentence.

Snoopy found the bone.

Whew.

Chances are that the child had never heard of a "glutch" before; yet he could readily form a plural. We characterize this ability as the *knowledge of a linguistic rule*. The child cannot state the rule (no more than he typically can state the rules of simple arithmetic), but he easily can use it. Linguistic theory can give us an exact statement of this plural rule that describes the "system" that underlies the child's language behavior. Such a rule would account for most regular plural formations in English (including sound variations between such words as "cat" or "fez" when pluralized). The child had some trouble, by contrast, with the "rule" for making active sentences out of passives. Again we could turn to linguistics to characterize the rule that relates active and passive syntactic forms of a sentence in English.

Rules guide our interpretation of sentences as well as their creation. Think for a moment about the meanings of these sentences:

Old men and women like to play cards.
Visiting relatives can be a nuisance.
They are flying planes.

These sentences cause problems for us because they have multiple meanings. (Both old men *and* old women or old men and *all* women? Are you going to see the relatives, or are they with you? Who is flying planes, or are they simply planes that fly?) That you can sense these alternative meanings is an example of how you are applying your knowledge of linguistic structure (again, *rules*). Notice here how these rules apply in alternative ways for each sentence, prompting alternative meanings.

In Chomsky's linguistic theory, rules are used to describe all the basic semantic, syntactic, and sound regularities (and interrelationships) of a language. Some of these rules are universal to all languages (for example, the basic qualities of sentence form), but many are specific to each language. These rules in Chomsky's terms, are called a *grammar* (a more specialized use of the term than is usual in "grammar" books). Linguists develop grammars, i.e., linguistic descriptions. Psychologists can refer to the grammar for types of rules that seem apparent in a child's language behavior.

When children learn language, we say they have developed a knowledge of the rules; that is, they have learned the grammar. This knowledge is given the specialized label of *competence* in linguistic theory. To summarize:

1. Modern linguistics sees the essence of language as a body of rules.
2. A body of rules is called a grammar.
3. A person's knowledge of a grammar is called linguistic competence.

Chomsky's linguistic theory usually is called a *generative grammar,* because one thinks of linguistic rules as the dynamic underpinnings of the creation or understanding of sentences. That is, if we choose to analyze a sentence, we can consider the rules necessary for its creation or understanding. We are not sure of the psychological form these rules take in our everday language behavior, but we can describe language theoretically pretty well with them. Note the generative quality in the following simplified example of a sentence construction.

$$\text{sentence} \longrightarrow \text{noun phrase} + \text{verb phrase}$$
$$\text{noun phrase} \longrightarrow \text{article} + \text{noun}$$
$$\text{verb phrase} \longrightarrow \text{verb} + \text{noun phrase}$$

With these rules we can provide a simplified account of one basic, English sentence structure. You might be familiar with it from high school sentence diagrams:

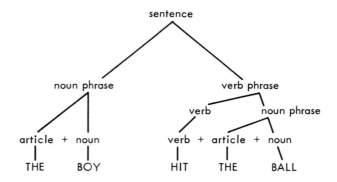

Although we have touched only the surface of linguistic theory, our examples give you an idea of the approach of generative grammar. The rule concept is vital, especially since nearly all that follows assumes that children's language develops as a system of rules. Our introduction to linguistic theory was meant primarily to give you an idea of what we mean by "rules."

PSYCHOLOGICAL THEORY

A few paragraphs ago we may have confused you by talking about linguistic competence (a person's knowledge of their language) and then saying we are not sure how linguistic rules are found in behavior. The concept of competence is theoretical. In fact it might be compared to mathematical theory in that such theory is related to our explanations of the bases for addition or subtraction. When we do simple arithmetic however, we do not draw directly from mathematical theory in our immediate behavior. We have learned how to add and to subtract as a pattern of strategies or methods of calculation. We think that it works somewhat this way for language. Our knowledge of language reflects the whole system of rules, yet we develop all sorts of strategies for carrying out these rules in everyday behavior. Psychological theories of language try to describe how we use competence, how it "enters into" performance. But this too, is a controversial topic in the contemporary study of child language. A number of good arguments can be made that we never can separate competence from performance sufficiently in research and that such separation may be all but impossible in studies of children.

Although it may seem that we are going off the deep end in talking about theory, considerations of competence and performance have helped the study of child language. Formerly, much study of child language was focused on performance—how many different things can a child say? Now we give some attention to competence—what, theoretically, children learn to be able to create and understand the sentences of their language? This question may yield much more fundamental answers than "how many different things can a child say?"

Nonetheless, to study child language we typically must consider situations of behavior. As already mentioned, much attention formerly was given to the stimulating and reinforcing conditions surrounding children's speech. In the new view of language, it is much more important to consider the linguistic experiences of a child and to try to determine just how a child can deduce the rules of the language from these experiences. Somehow this capability for deducing rules is a feature of the human brain. Humans seem to come equipped for developing linguistic rules; probably the most fundamental rules are those that comprise the universals of language. The environment then serves up experiences in French, English, or Swahili that are the bases for deducing specific rules of a language.

Motivation does not seem to play as important a role as traditionally thought. What seem particularly important are linguistic *experience* plus active *participation* in that experience. The concept of linguistic rules becomes especially useful when we consider what it is that a child learns when he learns language. How is the rule deduced from experience? (and what experience?); what, actually, does the child learn? Psychologists studying such questions have drawn heavily from theory in generative grammar. Two lines of reasoning have emerged particularly. First, it was argued that the new linguistic theory was so persuasive that any psychological theory of child language development should take it into account. Second, a great deal of critical rethinking was undertaken concerning the traditional view of language. For example:

If a typical five-year-old had to have experienced previously everything he or she could say, it would take an incredible amount of time (one estimate was five times the age of the earth!)

Except when somebody is trying to direct a child to imitate an utterance, children typically do not spend much time in sheer imitation activities.

When children do repeat something, they do not imitate exactly the sounds they hear. That is, they do not imitate as a parrot does. They tend to paraphrase in terms of basic sound segments and patterns of the language—the same phenomenon that gives them an accent when repeating a word or phrase in a foreign language. It is as if a child internalizes a set of rules for sound patterns and applies them when putting together new words or phrases. (Parrots have no such capability. They more directly imitate what they hear and thus have no accent carryovers unless what they imitate is itself accented.)

When children repeat something, they usually do not imitate the exact syntactic pattern. More often they paraphrase the essence of a statement in their own reduced syntactic version (e.g., "Daddy is going now" ⟶ "Daddy go"). This also is as if a child internalizes a set of rules—in this case for syntactic patterns.

The foregoing observations have focused on the child's *active* role as a language learner. There are several good arguments that this active role for acquiring language proceeds as does any other type of basic growth—according to a built-in or biologically based schedule. Studies of brain development, based on chemical measures of growth, show that for each stage we can detect changes in language development. Also, as we compare child language development across the diverse cultures and tongues of the world, it seems that all children go through similar stages of language development. Thus, contrary to our own problems with high school French, all stages of language develop at about the same rate in children and in about the same way that self-feeding, walking, and adolescence develop at certain ages in children of all cultures.

Contemporary psychological studies of language behavior are so influenced by modern linguistic theory that we often refer to them as *psycholinguistic* studies.

SOCIOLOGICAL THEORY

Most psychological studies of performance are a few steps removed from studies of everyday speech behavior, particularly from those that take into account the vast differences among individual speakers. Until the 1960s there was not much interest in the study of everyday speech or in the diversity in and among individual speakers of a language. Traditional linguistics and even generative grammar focus largely on statements of uniformity about language patterns, in contrast to theorizing about diversity itself. Certainly, in any speaker, or among speakers, a vast number of generalizations can be developed about basic linguistic rules. But within a rule system of a language, people do differ. Children differ from adults. Ethnic and regional groups differ. Social status groups differ. Even individuals differ in their speech in terms of a great number of practical factors—to whom they are talking, topic, their emotional state, and so on. The study of everyday speech differences has received particular impetus in the United States in the contemporary work of William Labov. He, in contrast to many contemporary linguists, has seen speech diversity as a critical topic for study. It reveals the practical and functional use of speech in everday situations, as well as giving us insights into the nature of linguistic evolution.

Although such studies of diversity as those by Labov are somewhat at theoretical odds with those of the generative grammarians, we believe that practical studies of language differences are a vital part of the new

view of language. They enable us to understand the nature of dialect—to see how the linguistic variations we detect in minority group children are predictable, legitimate characteristics. They enable us to see how children's practical use of speech develops across time. And particularly important, practical studies of diversity aid us in characterizing children's speech as a functional, living thing—rather than concentrating solely upon abstract, underlying theoretical concepts.

Consider, for example, this segment of an interview with six-year-old Mary Beth. It illustrates how, in a very short time on this earth, a child becomes capable of manipulating the fundamentals of language with functional ease (and of carrying on an interesting conversation at the same time!).

That's right; you have two mother cats, don't you?

Mary Beth: Yes.

What are the names of the mother cats?

Um . . . Marisha and Kung Fu.

And they're the ones that are . . . had the baby kittens?

Yes. Kung Fu had three kittens, but one of hers had the disease and it died.

What happened to that little kitten that you had that was walking crooked all the time?

He wasn't walking crooked. All . . . when I came to see you . . . ah . . . I wa . . . ah . . . Sonny didn't know he was dead, but I came to the little house . . . the green one . . . and . . . and . . . and he . . . and he . . . And when I came over here I couldn't find him. I thought he was under . . . you know . . . there's a little porch and I thought he was under there, but . . . and then I looked this way and then he was dead. I saw him dead. And I went to go and call my brother . . . on his . . .

But didn't you have a kitten before that was a little older and that used to walk crooked?

Yes.

What was his name?

Chato.

It was Chato! What did he die of, Mary Beth?

Well . . . he got runned over.

Oh, he did? By whom?

By my father.

Oh, your father ran over him.

Yes, he doesn't watch where he's going.

That's why he was runned over?

Yeah.

Do you miss Chato?

Yes. And I miss my cat . . . and you put him outside!

How did you know your father ran over him?

Sonny told me. Be . . . cause he was runned over and the eyes popped out.

Did you bury him?

Yes. I put a cross on him and Sonny put up . . . put up the cross on top of my house.

Oh, so the cross doesn't stand on his grave anymore?

It stands on there, but he pulls 'em out and puts 'em in my window.

Oh, in your little playhouse?

Yeah.

Did you tell him that you wanted the cross back on the grave?

No. But I'll tell him.*

Modern sociological, or *sociolinguistic,* methods provide us with insights into the analysis of Mary Beth's speech. For one thing, her speech is generally representative for a child her age. She uses the linguistic rules used by most six-year-olds and even misuses the same ones ("runned over"). In listening to her speech sample, you will notice that it had a slight accent—"sh" sounds (as in "shoe" have a "ch" quality (as in "choo"); the "s" in a word like "position" comes out more hissed than voiced; the "i" in "him" sounds somewhat like "heem." Mary Beth is a Mexican-American child with some carry-over into her English from Spanish. It is largely a sound carry-over, however; so it is not found in the transcript.

Perhaps you noted how functional Mary Beth's speech was. Although she was talking about things that could upset her, she kept her speech relatively separate from her emotions, except perhaps when talking about her first kitten. She was doing a good job of answering the interviewer's questions, including injecting a comment of her own when her cat was put out.

In listening to Mary Beth you might form some attitudes about her. As we said, her speech is accented; so perhaps this will elicit some attitudes about her being Mexican-American. Her speech is, at the same time, confident and eager, even when describing her lost pets.

All of the foregoing—the study of child differences in speech, functional aspects of conversation, and even linguistic attitudes—are parts of the new view of language furnished by sociological studies.

THE INTEGRATED VIEW

Most of what we have discussed thus far has been an introduction to three major aspects of the new view of language, namely:

*Smaller type indicates conversation not included in recording.

How can we characterize what a child learns when he or she learns
language? (Linguistic aspect.)

How can we characterize the cognitive and behavioral operations
necessary for the use of language? (Psychological aspect.)

How can we characterize how a child's language may vary according
to social factors? (Sociological aspect.)

Given these brief introductions, the next important consideration is
that in most new views of children's speech the linguistic, psychological, and
sociological aspects are considered simultaneously. To draw inferences about
what a child has learned of language, we must observe behavior with
language. To interpret that behavior we must also assess it relative to social
factors. Even if the emphasis of a study is on the social variation of language,
there still will be a delineation of the language performance itself in
linguistic terms. If the emphasis is upon hypotheses about cognitive
operations involved in language behavior, there still will be a linguistic
specification of what aspect of language the child is trying to use. Although
the following chapters focus on relatively different topics concerning child
language, you'll notice soon that they typically draw in varying degrees
upon the linguistic, psychological, and sociological aspects of language
study.

This integrated view characterizes current trends in thinking and
research in child language.[1] From the linguistic aspect, the assumption is
that a child develops a rule system for language. This is based on a
psychological capability associated with the biological heritage to develop
language. This psychological capability combined with a sociocultural
environment that provides exposure and interaction with a specific language
leads to language development.

Some of the most productive contemporary studies of child language
stress a child's *semantic* development, which in many ways ties together
linguistic, psychological, and social factors. Very early in this chapter we
defined language as the knowledge of relations between sounds and
meanings. Studies that emphasize semantic development attempt to capture
objectively how a child's meanings develop and how those meanings relate
to the sounds we can observe in his or her speech. Thus, it becomes
important to study such highly functional and realistic speech situations as
mother-and-child conversations, where we can make good guesses about
what the child presumably is talking about. The challenge is that a child's
meanings appear to develop in ever-increasing patterns of complexity, as do
the patterns of speech itself. Because a child's system of language is not a
miniature version of an adult system, however, we must *not* imply that
a child has the exact same meanings that we might assign to a particular

---

[1] Roger Brown's excellent volume, *First Language* (Harvard University Press, 1973)
is a major example of such trends.

utterance. There is the goal, therefore, not only to try to determine the kinds of meanings relevant to a child but also to find how sound patterns of speech at a particular age reflect associations with those meanings. Such approaches have resulted in a number of attempts to define linguistic structures as they may emerge in terms of semantic functions in child speech—for example, simple designation of objects or events, the modification of these designations, differences in basic sentence forms, and inter-relations of sentences.

The picture of the developing child that emerges in the new view of language is that of *meaning in search of expression.* Children are active experimenters with language, and most language is learned in everyday, functional communication behaviors that are relevant to the life of a child. This new view underlies the philosophy of this book—that our main role as adults is to create optimum conditions in which children can experience and interact with the language of their environment.

SOME CONCLUDING NOTES

This is a nontechnical book. We are more interested in giving you a broad survey of the practical aspects of child language development and of child language differences than one of theoretical insights. On the other hand, if this practical view whets your appetite for more information, there are carefully suggested references for further reading in the back of the book.

Here are some notes on the remaining chapters.

Chapter 2.   Given the threefold introduction to the new view of language in Chapter 1, this chapter summarizes some of the contemporary thinking on the nature of language development in more detail. We have concentrated upon generalizations that are now in favor with most theorists and that should have practical value in your own work with child language. Most of the materials reflect the psycholinguistic approach that began in the 1960s but include some of the more basic aspects of the semantic approaches of the mid-1970s.

Chapter 3.   One of the most salient characteristics of language, particularly in such a heterogeneous population as that of the United States, is that all children do not sound alike. We have what linguists call social and regional dialects. By *dialect* we mean that the people speak the same language and are intelligible to one another but that there are easily recognizable differences among groups of speakers. One of the key points in our chapter on social and regional dialects is that there are quite legitimate and logical variations in human language. We should avoid equating dialects that are not in the mainstream language of a country as with something more "simple" or "underdeveloped." In America, for example, there is a great variety of dialects, and so-called standard English is simply one of those dialects. The fact that some occupations require standard English is more a consequence of social attitudes than of anything having to do with linguistics.

Chapter 4.   Particularly in the last decade in the United States, linquists and pscyhologists have given increased attention to some of the major ethnic dialects of English. One of these, variously known as Black English, Negro nonstandard, or American Black, has been the subject of considerable study. During the 1960s there were various academic arguments over whether black dialect was a language separate from English or simply a dialect. Although many will argue this point, if there is any emerging consensus it is that black English is a dialect probably more marked from or at more variance with standard English than are most other dialects. Yet its variance is not so great that speakers of Black English and those of so-called standard English cannot usually understand one another.

Chapter 5.   There always has been a substantial amount of attention given to the influence of one language upon another. In the United States one particular topic has been the influence of Spanish upon English, and vice versa. If we view the characteristics of both languages in general it is not difficult to predict the kinds of variations in English to expect from a native speaker of Spanish (or, by the same token, the variations in Spanish to expect from a native speaker of English). In the 1960s, as educators began to awaken to the challenge of the many students in American schools whose primary language was Spanish, substantial attention began to be given to the Spanish influence on English. This has necessitated additional attention to some of the variations of Spanish found among, for example, Mexican-Americans, Puerto Ricans, and Cubans. As with the Black dialect, the fact that a person speaking English may have a number of Spanish interferences does not typically inhibit intelligibility.

Chapter 6.   Some language characteristics are socially significant because of the attitudes they elicit in people. We have summarized some of the main aspects of language attitudes such as those found in studies involving teachers. If the thought has occurred to you that this has something like a Pygmalion effect, you are indeed correct. It may be the case that how a child *sounds* may cause a teacher to *feel* a certain way toward that pupil. The teacher's instruction may likewise be affected, and perhaps how well a child does in school becomes a self-fulfilling prophecy.

And we have gone a step further than simply providing a summary of the various aspects of the new view of language. We have added implications where possible on what the new view suggests in the way of practical ideas for dealing with the language of children.

The Sounds of Children's Speech

2

Brian (age 5): Dolphin, dolphin, dolphin 34. Dolphin, don't! Look at the dolphin right at the spot in the air. Dolphin, don't! Don't! No, no, dolphin! Dripping spring. No, no, dolphin. No no!

Ooo. I'm on the "freet" board, what am I doing on the freet board? Rain, rain go away. Come again some other day. That's what you were doing on the freet board. Now, it's time for the real dolphin contest. She's been talking she's gotta get down. She has to get the toughies, she got a teamwork. She got really does me too. Got two gangs . . . is what he's got.

Christine (age 18 months): Oooh. It's still wet. Cause still fall down. Ooo we, I got one dry Brian. Eee I got, its his nose go "dop!"

LEARNING TO TALK

Brian and Christine are playing in the bathtub. They also are learning to talk. In the new view of language, such play as these two children demonstrate may be the most vital form of "talking practice." What could be more natural, or more fun!

The new view of language brings a whole new perspective to child's speech development. As mentioned in Chapter 1, some scholars dispute whether the child really learns to talk. Rather, it is claimed that a child simply grows up talking, that this is a distinctive behavior pattern for man just as spinning webs is for spiders. Speech grows out of the child himself in as natural a way as learning to walk. The child speaks or is classified as abnormal if he does not. A nondeaf child of deaf-mute parents learns to speak; an immigrant child learns the new language fluently if any of his playmates speak it; a child of parents who rarely talk may grow up to be talkative.

Children do not need to "practice" language to learn it in the sense that one must practice playing the piano, shooting baskets or sewing. For example, Eric Lenneberg reports the case of a child who made no babbling sounds from the age of 8 months to 14 months because his voice had been silenced by a throat operation. When the child's voice was restored his sounds were typical of his age group, in spite of the "babbling practice" he had missed.

Do you feel that babbling practice is important to normal speech and language development? We can understand how you might feel that way, since in the old view of language development babbling was considered a major building stage. More recently, researchers have found it less important. Children who babble very little apparently are unhindered in later development. Children babble some sounds that are not used in words until five years later. Babbling's main use seems to be for practicing intonation patterns that will be used later in sentences.

Finally, the development of language and speech emerges in a fairly set sequence that runs roughly parallel to that of motor skills. Children babble at about the same time they learn to sit up and use the thumb in grasping objects (five-seven months). They learn their first words and respond to simple commands at about the same time they take those first halting steps (10-18 months). They attain a rapidly increasing working vocabulary at about the same time they learn to run and climb stairs (24-30 months). We caution you not to take such stages too literally. Children do not develop according to infallible schedules. A child who falls a few months behind the dates listed here is not retarded. The important point is that speech and motor aspects develop at roughly the same time—a child with a large vocabulary who cannot walk or one who runs but rarely speaks would be unusual and perhaps a candidate for therapy.

In sum, children's speech development is based on a biological schedule. Children in different countries, or those who spring from widely diverse environments, seem to discover capacities for speech in much the same ways. For example, most two-year-olds all over the world use word order in two- and three-word utterances to signal meaning. This is the case even when they are learning languages in which word order is not too important to adult speech. Russian and German, for instance, are inflected in adult speech, and word order is less important. Yet children learning these languages still use word order for grammar in the early stages.

If this biological view of language is correct, then attempts by parents and teachers to teach children how to talk seem superfluous. Children learn to talk by listening, by talking, and above all, by playing at it. That a child's play is a cornerstone of his language development is illustrated by the following conversations. Note the many creative utterances spoken by these children that are unlikely ever to have been spoken by adults. Here and throughout this book, note, too, how much more eloquent children become when they *actively participate* in conversations.

Brian (age 6): Hey, let's play zoo.

Brad (age 8): I'm the zoo keeper, you two are the monkeys.

Brett (age 6): I'm the monkey, we're different animals in here, and we fight! I'm a tiger, you're a lion.

Brian: Uh-uh, I'm a gorilla.

Brad: Hey! Hey, I have an idea.

Brett: I'm a monkey.

Brad: Hey I have idea; see a monkey is a gorilla's son.

Brian: (to Brad, who is hitting him) Gorillas don't hurt monkeys. Listen, gorillas don't hurt monkeys.

Brett: Gorillas are monkeys and they both fight (screeches).

Brad: Don't, Brett, you're gonna hurt him. The zoo keeper's gonna get ya!

Brett: You gotta be an animal. You can't get in here, or you're trapped.

Brian: Uh-huh, because the zoo keeper goes in cages.

Brad: Yeah, and to stop fights, too.

Brian: I'm one of the zoo keeper's helpers.

Brett: I'm the monkey.

Brian: Getting in a fight with a monkey is tough when you're the zoo keeper's helper.

Brad: Be a good monkey, OK?

Brian: I take care of most of the things and I stay in the cages and stuff like that . . . I gotta read my checklist . . . Quit it, quit it (animal noises). That one's mine. That one's mine.

Brad: That monkey's fetching it.

Brian: Or he's a three-way dog.

Children learn a great deal from creative make-believe. Any parent is humbled when he or she hears a child play "Mommy and Daddy," showing the parent from the child's point of view. The next selection shows an even more obvious form of performance.

> *Whole group of children* (age 6): It's my turn (several times).
> *Elizabeth:* I'll make you cry.
> *Mary Beth:* My turn.
> *Elizabeth:* My turn, OK, OK your turn and then my turn.
> *Mary Beth:* OK, I'm gonna sing, "He's Able."

He's able, He's able, I know He's able.
I know my Lord is able t' carry me through.
(Repeats first two lines.)
He helped the broken hearted.
And let the "captains" free.
And made the "lamb" to walk again,
And caused the blind to see.
He's able (first two lines repeated).
Sing it again, Okay? Do it real good, Okay? Everybody . . . everybody . . .
    everybody sing,
Okay? No. just me sing and all you play your arms when I sing this, Okay?
    Um, I'm gonna sing a song. Okay.
He's able (repeats first two lines).
I'm gonna get something. You be saying something, Okay?

WHAT IS LEARNED?

A biological view of communication development emphasizes how all children develop in similar ways. Yet some people are more similar to you than others. Some people speak languages that are unintelligible to you. Your common biological heritage does not magically allow you to understand one another. Rather, each child learns to speak English or Russian while hearing other people speak it. That is not quite the same as saying that those other people teach them how. The authors once knew a three-year-old French child whose parents had been in the United States for two months and were soon going home. They wanted their child to learn no English for fear it would damage his properly learning French (a baseless fear). These parents instructed other adults not to address the child in English, so he would not learn it. But this child chattered fluent English with his peers on the playground when his mother left him alone. He not only knew how to speak English; he also knew his mother didn't like him speaking it!

Children do *learn* to talk in the sense that they only speak languages to which they are exposed and in which they participate in communicating.

Yet they learn while playing, so quickly and almost effortlessly that they could be considered "experts" in language analysis. It seems ironic that a four-year-old who has learned thousands of intricacies about his language and can converse with mature adults is still usually unable to tie his shoes. *Different skills are learned in different ways at different speeds.*

Practically the slowest kind of learning is pure rote memorization. Most people who have attended college have served as subjects for psychology experiments in which they were asked to memorize difficult and meaningless lists of words or pairs of nonsense syllables. In contrast, a poem, a joke, or an exciting story can be learned quite quickly, because it has meaningful structure and because the learner is more likely to find it interesting. In this sense, different aspects of learning to talk proceed at different rates. Children can memorize principles of grammar only with difficulty (in spite of the efforts of many teachers), because those principles seem like sterile lists of trivia. Yet children can *apply* such principles with fluent ease, because by doing so they establish contact with others and are able to communicate what is on their minds.

With this background, here are a few facts about the learning strategies that children employ in acquiring communication skills.

Memorization, practice, and rote imitation.   To the surprise of some parents, these forms of learning seem of little importance to language development. Children do often "echo," and such utterances attract enough attention that they may seem a major part of the child's speech. Such occurrences, however, are not as common as they sometimes seem; and they do not materially affect learning to talk. The major memorized aspects of speech are vocabulary growth, idioms, and pronunciation features that are often characteristic of dialects. These are important items but not ones central to learning to talk, according to the new view of language.

Rewarding good performance.   Adults tend to reward some utterances of children. The first infant utterances that sound like "mama" are rewarded with squeals of delight from parents. Similar rewards for "bye-bye," "please," and for naming objects ("truck," "doggie") sometimes create an impression that parents teach children how to talk by rewarding speech behaviors. This view is sufficiently attractive to be the basis for a behaviorist view of language learning.

Such a theory is undoubtedly a good explanation of the child's first few words. Studies by psycholinguist Roger Brown and his colleagues, however, have shown that parents do not *consistently* reward the child's use of new and complex grammar structures—something they would *have* to do to teach them to speak with a reward system. Rather, parents reward utterances that have true meanings and that are situationally appropriate, whether they are grammatical or not. A parent would be likely to reward the child who said,

"Me four year old,"

if she is four. But parents would *corrent* the same child if she said,

"I will be three years old tomorrow,"

since she is not going to be three. Similarly, a parent would smile and give a positive response to a moral but grammatically flawed statement:

"Jesus love childs."

but not to a grammatically complex, well-executed statement of questionable content:

"My friend Julie showed me her bottom today."

In summary, parents teach their children ethics, appropriateness, and correct meanings of utterances—but not sentence structure or the sound system of a language.

Rule-induction.   Perhaps the most important learning process in children's speech development is a sort of jumping to conclusions. Based on the speech he hears and the utterances he receives reinforcement for speaking, the child inductively makes guesses about the structure of his language. This is a powerful variety of generalization learning. On the basis of such learning, the child often speaks sentences of annoying length and complexity. On his second birthday, Brian Hopper spoke his first sentence of more than three words:

"Brian's gonna be a tiger, Daddy."

Soon afterward, he said to his mother,

"When I'm a father, you will be a grandmother."

Such sentences are far more complex than most that were produced, and they illustrate some excellent "guesses" about language structure. Such guesses—undertaken with minimal supporting data—are overgeneralizations that sometimes prove accurate, sometimes inaccurate. Overgeneralized rule-induction accounts for many of the quaint errors that are so characteristic of a young child's speech. It is common for a two-year-old to learn such

words as "bow-wow" or "doggie" to refer to the four-legged animal that serves as man's best friend. Soon this word appears in reference to nearly *all* four-legged animals, as well as to occasional bicycles and cars. Only over time does the child begin to distinguish various four-legged animals from each other and from other moving things.

Similar errors of overgeneralization appear in the grammatical structure of children's speech. Irregular verbs, for example, often are used in "over-regularized" forms, because children overgeneralize the rules for regular verbs. This produces "I runned," "She goed," and "He falled down." Similar overregularizations of noun inflections produce "foots," "mans," and "mouses." An ironic aspect of these overgeneralizations is that children usually use irregular verbs and nouns correctly when they first learn them. They apparently are imitated or memorized. When children inductively learn the regular endings, however, the irregular endings are displaced in spite of having been practiced. This event has been dubbed *inflectional imperialism* by psycholinguist Dan Slobin, and it serves as evidence that rule induction is more relied upon by children than is memory or practice. Overgeneralized utterances are children's own inventions. They certainly do not hear them from adults; they construct them from their own linguistic generalizations. The creative nature of these generalizations often is shown in sentences that put meanings together in totally new ways. One boy, who apparently had learned his ecology lessons well, said:

"Mommy, I love you a thousand trees."

In sum, rule-governed generalization is perhaps the strongest learning strategy used by the child for language development. The learning sequence goes something like this: first, the child discovers some meaning, or task to be performed; he or she simultaneously gleans from the surroundings a new item of code that speakers use in apparent conjunction with that meaning or task. The child then overgeneralizes the function of the newly discovered piece of code by applying it to some larger class of wants. Given that the child's code has fewer items than there are items in the world, many things the child says will appear (to adults) to be rather quaint errors. The child then sorts mixed feedback to learn more specific rules—that also are to be overgeneralized. Each cycle of overgeneralization and discrimination creates language categories that are more specific, reality centered, and useful. This process seems to be the key in most children's learning of speech sounds and sentence structure.

Although this discussion of learning strategies emphasizes the importance of rule-induction—two limitations to this argument deserve mention. First, the process of linguistic rule-induction is difficult to understand, let alone control. Pointing out its importance does not suggest that anyone understands in detail how it works. We are even less certain about what kinds of teaching strategies can best aid such development. The essence of any such strategy, however, seems to be that children need to talk and to be listened to—to engage in the give-and-take of genuine, interesting, relevant conversation. That is not always easy to arrange within the confines of a classroom and of the requirements for discipline. However, it certainly argues against the advisability of a classroom in which teachers talk and children are silent most of the time.

The second qualification is that each child is different. Some children are quick to generalize, others less so. Some children imitate adult speech a good deal, others less. Some children are able to make quick use of feedback from others, other children seem to ignore such feedback. Each child develops some of his or her own learning strategies. No two children learn to talk in precisely the same way.

It follows that teachers and parents should not try to teach language—in the same way to all children. How can they adjust to each child? By listening—by listening for the child's own style of making "errors" with the goal of *understanding* that system, rather than correcting it.

Please examine the transcripts of three samples of child speech that appear below. These illustrate children actively engaged in learning to talk. What is the child learning in each case? How can you tell?

Dad: Did Christine eat breakfast?

Christine (18 months): Yes.

Dad: Eggs?

Chris: Eggs.

Dad: With Brian?

Chris: "Maya" (Brian).

Dad: And Mom?

Chris: Mom.

Dad: And Dad?

Chris: Daddy.

Dad: And Christine?

Chris: Christine.

Dad: Christine was there, sure.

Chris: Christine there.

Dad: Christine was in her pajamas.

Chris: Christine "nammies."

Dad: Right, and she ate egg.

Chris: Egg.

Dad: With cheese.

Chris: Cheese.

Dad: And she ate toast.

Chris: Toast . . . and cheese?

Dad: With her fork.

Chris: "Vook," "vook" (fork).

Dad: Um-hum, do you think today you'll play with Kerri?

Chris: "Dooie?"[1]

Dad: And Doug?

Chris: Doug.

Dad: And Brian?

Chris: "Maya."

Dad: And Julie? (Another friend, not to be confused with Kerri-"Dooie".)

Chris: Julie.

Dad: And Kerri?

Chris: "Dooies."

Dad: And Kerri's Mommy?

Chris: Mommy.

Dad: Is Kerri's Mommy the same as your Mommy?

Chris: My Mommy, and Dooies (unintelligible) no more.

Dad: Um, what do you play?
Chris: "Dooies."
Dad: At her house?
Chris: House
Dad: Will you swing?
Chris: Yes.
Dad: Will you swing way up high?
Chris: Yeh.
Dad: What will you do in the sand box?
Chris: Do the sand box.
Dad: You build with toys?
Chris: Yes, I build with toys.
Dad: What kind of toys, trucks?
Chris: Truck.

You probably observed that Christine was imitating. It is worth re-emphasizing that all children develop their own strategies for learning to talk. For many children, imitation seems relatively unimportant; but Christine habitually engaged in so much apparently productive imitation that she must be considered an exception.

[1] Imitation is not simply rote sound; Christine regularly called her friend Kerri by the name "Dooie" for several months.

This fact leads us to considerations of the general role of parents in fostering development. Much of this chapter has emphasized the biological nature of communication development, which makes it seem that the parent has little role. In a sense this is true—we have no way of knowing whether any particular actions of parents help or hinder a child's development. A series of studies in the past few years has consistently shown, however, that there are relationships between the general interaction patterns of parents (especially the mother) and the child's communication development. It is worthwhile to review some of these findings in detail.

The most consistent finding has been that the speech of adults to young children is simpler in structure and content than is their speech to older children and to other adults. Differences were even observed between mothers' speech to 28-month-old children and to 18-month-old children. Most adults (and most children) are aware of "baby talk," but these observations go far beyond that. Adults use shorter sentences (three-four words) and more repetition when talking to young children. We cannot say for certain that this aids development, but such simplified speech does seem an ideal instructional tool.

An important feature of simplified speech to children is its naturalness. Nonparents seem to do it as well (and instinctively) as do experienced parents. It happens effortlessly. Even children are aware of it. Four-year-olds even simplify their speech when speaking to two-year-olds.

Chances are that parents who try to make their speech most appropriate to their child's level will get tangled in their own tongues; whereas, if people just allow themselves to adjust naturally to the situation the level chosen probably will be appropriate. One study showed the futility of the usual parent-teacher attempts to influence children's behavior. The experimenters observed children playing with two toys. In a second session, the experimenter drew the children's attention to the toy they had played with *least;* and this toy was discussed. Subsequent observation showed that the children played with this toy even *less* after the "lesson."

The parent and teacher behaviors that have been found most effective in fostering development are rather intuitive things that nearly every parent knows about: expressing affection for the child, accepting the child's behavior, and offering socially stimulating conversation. The *particulars* of how such feelings are expressed may differ with subcultural background. For example, studies have shown that Mexican-American and Chinese-American parents expect more deference to authority than do other American parents. Similarly, Black children show more physical attachment to their mothers than do most other groups in the United States. Some mothers are most interested in *teaching,* which makes school success somewhat more likely. But the general, global behaviors that are productive of development seem to hold equally in almost all cultural groups. When the child is accepted and cherished as a person who has something to contribute to human interaction, his or her development is enhanced.

When the child is considered a possession of the parents who must behave in certain ways to insure parental happiness, the consequences are less certain.

The next sample illustrates a type of parent-child conversation that can be immensely profitable in terms of the child's learning to communicate. Six-year-old Mary Beth talks to her mother.

Mary Beth: Uh, Mom, um, what would happen if you had one more baby?

Mom: Oh my goodness, don't even think about it any.

Mary Beth: What would happen if . . . ?

Mom: You know what's gonna happen, you're not gonna be the baby.

Mary Beth: I know, that's good, cause I don't like to be the baby.

Mom: Why?

Mary Beth: Cause . . . I hate to be the baby around the house.

Mom: I thought you liked it all the time.

Mary Beth: I don't.

Mom: Well, Cindy pampers you too much. Daddy does, too.

Mary Beth: I know . . . I would like to have two little brothers.

Mom: Two little brothers?

Mary Beth: Yeah, because, I . . . I have a mother and father, they go together, and tie, right?

Mom: Uh huh.

Mary Beth: Well, there's one boy and two girls, right?

Mom: Um hum.

Mary Beth: You don't know what I mean.

Mom: Yes, I know what you mean.

Mary Beth: Look, this is Daddy.

Mom: A pair.

Mary Beth: Daddy and Mama, right?

Mom: Uh huh.

Mary Beth: Okay, um, there's more girls than boys.

Mom: Uh-hum, you need two boys, huh? I see.

Mary Beth: Uh-hum.

Mom: But Bethy, don't you stop to think that I'm getting old?

Mary Beth: No! as long as the kids aren't getting married, then they're not old.

Mom: (laughs) That's why I'm not old, because you're not married?

> *Mary Beth:* Yeah.
> *Mom:* Oh, Bethy . . .

The key to the conversation between Mary Beth and her mother is the degree to which they participate as equals in the thought process. The next tape illustrates a more common learning situation among genuine equals—three children in a quarrel over toys.

> *Brian* (age 6): Can I have the jar, please, Brad? Now, no more keeping nails over there.
> *Brad* (age 8): This . . .
> *Brian:* Your brother did it!
> *Brett* (age 6): (Hammers) Can I have another nail?
> *Brian:* No.
> *Brett:* Brad gots another one.
> *Brian:* Well . . .
> *Brad:* Well, that's the last one I'm gonna get.
> *Brett:* Why can't I have another one?
> *Brian:* Because you kept the nails closer to you.
> *Brett:* No I didn't, I kept them right there.
> *Brian:* And that was close to you, and you should have brought 'em back over to me.
> *Brad:* Hey Brian, next time . . . okay.
> *Brett:* I'm leaving. I'm going home, and say, Bri! And shut up, cause I'm not ever coming over here again.
> *Brian:* I'm gonna get you a nail in a minute.
> *Brett:* I'm leaving, I don't care! (Cries.)
> *Brad:* Okay, then I won't.
> *Brett:* I'm gonna get my wood, and I'm gonna throw it down your face and kill you!

Sometimes the sense of participation that children get from fighting and playing can be provided by thoughtful and well-prepared teachers in classroom settings. This deserves to be a goal of communication instruction.

PRESCHOOL CHILDREN'S LANGUAGE DEVELOPMENT

The past 15 years have witnessed an explosion of research in a field that often is called *developmental psycholinguistics.* Students of developmental psycholinguistics ordinarily are most interested in the acquisition of the verbal language code by very young children—the genesis of language.

Most such research has drawn from the theory and terminology of generative transformational grammar and has traced the child's development in terms of:

1. The sound system (*phonology*).
2. The sentence structure (*syntax*).
3. The meaning (*semantics*) of what the child says.

Research studies of developmental psycholinguistics often have gone into great detail, although such details rarely become important to instruction. Still, some broad outlines of the child's early language development seem to be worth sketching.

Sounds.   The development of the sound system in young children's language long has been studied. Many recordings have been made of the babbling of babies, for example; and there have been attempts to establish some connection between the progress of babbling and later speech or language development. These attempts rarely have been successful. In fact, the phenomenon of babbling, which twenty years ago was considered central to the process of language learning, now is considered more or less unimportant. The babbling child often makes sounds that he/or she will not make again for five years. Children who do not babble do not seem to be handicapped in later development. The main value of babbling probably is that it gives the child practice in the intonation system of the language. If you listen to the advanced babbling and imitations of a 14-month-old child, you will recognize some characteristic patterns of sentence intonation that can be found in adult speech.

With "true speech"—speech using words—children seem to start all over again with sound development. Even though sounds have appeared in babbling, they still must be remastered for use in words. By age five, children have developed mastery of nearly all the sounds of the language in mature form, although some consistent mispronunciations and aberrations persist much later. A normal child may mispronounce the sounds "l" and "r" until age seven. Don't be in a hurry to think such children have a problem.

Syntax.   Sentence structure is the aspect of development that has been studied most by developmental psycholinguists. This seems slightly paradoxical, because the study of syntax might be the aspect of linguistics least relevant to educational practices. Syntax may be fairly irrelevant to classroom practices, because there seems little that intervention can do to alter the basic course of its development. Some studies have reported modest gains in the speed of syntactic development, but none of these differences has been sufficient to advocate teaching syntax in any conscious way.

The pioneer in syntax studies has been psycholinguist Roger Brown, who conducted a longitudinal study of the syntactic development of three children. He also has summarized most of what presently is known about the very young child's syntax development in an excellent and thorough book called *A First Language.* The major question that Brown addresses in his book is this: How much language can you give a child credit for when he speaks very short sentences—say, two words long?

This issue is important, because early syntax studies gave a child very little credit indeed. These studies supposed only that the child knew a very elementary set of rules for putting two words together and that to the child, every set of two words was much like every other set of two words. This position is called the *pivot grammar theory* of children's syntax development. The trouble with the pivot grammar theory is that children obviously intend more than simple meanings in two-word utterances and that the child can be understood clearly. For example, a child might say, "Mommy sock." This utterance might mean that the child has found a sock belonging to Mommy, or that she wants help from Mommy in putting on her own sock, or several other things. The point is that listeners usually have little difficulty understanding which of the meanings the child is trying to get across. Therefore, the child must know more about sentences than simply how to put two words together. The position that gives the child credit for knowing a lot more about syntax than does the pivot grammar approach is called the *theory of rich interpretation.*

Meaning.   The rich interpretation notion brings up another problem: What is the nature of what the child knows when he says simple utterances with rather complex meanings? The best answer is that the child really doesn't necessarily know a lot about syntax, but he does know a lot about meaning. Yet some parts of syntax are very close to *being* meaning. For example, generative transformational linguists use the term *deep structure* to refer to a part of syntax that is somewhat closer to meaning than the rest. Other linguists have argued that deep structure actually *is* meaning. Still other linguists have constructed theories of grammar called *case grammar* that use categories of meaning as organizers for language structure. The point is that the notion of rich interpretation (giving the child credit for knowing a lot when he says only a few words) blurs the line between syntax and semantics.

These details may not be particularly important to anything that happens in the classroom, but they may lead to educational innovations in the future. For now, the major implication of developmental psycholinguistic research with preschool children is this: The five-year-old child who enters kindergarten already has a fairly fully developed language system, and he has that system regardless of the nature of his environment (unless he was raised in a basement or under the care of wolves). There

does not seem to be much that teachers or parents can do about speeding up this development, even if such a thing were desirable. About the best advice is to relax and enjoy the child's youthful enthusiasm.

COMMUNICATION DEVELOPMENT
FROM KINDERGARTEN TO SIXTH GRADE

It is obvious to most people that sixth graders speak somewhat differently than do kindergartners. The new view of language makes the precise nature of those differences clearer than before. The most remarkable, recent finding is that the grammar of the kindergarten child is almost complete. The five-year-old has mastered most major syntactic rules of her language. Only a few exceptions to these rules remain to be learned. This means that many attempts to teach syntax in school may be superfluous.

To say that a five-year-old knows grammar is not, of course, to claim that she can diagram sentences. Nor is it to say that she never makes mistakes in her speech—everyone does. Finally, children often say, "ain't" or "they was" or "he had two shoe" or "I goed home"; but none of these is absolutely ungrammatical. Such utterances do follow linguistic rules, although their patterns of usage are unacceptable in some environments. The elementary school child *does* need training in acceptable patterns of usage. *The five-year-old knows a lot about grammar, but lacks training in acceptable usage and effective communication.* He is much like someone who knows how to play chess (knows the rules), yet would rarely win a game against an experienced player. In addition to knowing the rules, the experienced player also possesses some knowledge about what tactics and strategies are most effective in particular situations. An experienced communicator learns about verbal tactics and strategies that prove effective. In Chapter 1, we noted that linguists give the label *performance* to this part of the child's behavior. Knowledge about performance is not actually grammatical or linguistic knowledge but information about how to *apply* language to actual communication settings—or about how the details of language relate to the details of communication. This distinction between grammar and performance may seem like hair splitting; it is important only because effective performance is primarily what the elementary child needs to be taught. Performance knowledge is developed best through actual practice in speaking, listening, reading, writing. The child needs opportunities to talk and to have his effective talk bring change to develop into an effective oral communicator. He needs these opportunities even at the occasional risk of losing quiet and order in the classroom. *Children can only learn effective communication performance through practice in effective communication.*

One striking linguistic characteristic of the speech of a kindergarten child is the *immaturity of his sound system.* In particular, the sounds, "r," "l," and "s" develop into their consistent mature forms quite late. Commonly children do not pronounce these sounds reliably in adult ways until age seven or eight. A caution is in order about normative data on sound development. Children are not public transport vehicles—their time tables are not strict. A child of seven who consistently substitutes "th" for "s" probably will grow out of it. If several sounds ordinarily acquired earlier than this still cause difficulty, however, the child may be a candidate for minor speech therapy. (Most schools now provide access to a speech clinician who will give advice on such problems.)

To illustrate age differences in child speech, we include a sample of a midwestern man talking with his two sons. The boys are ages four and eight, and their speech (when compared with their father's) shows a counterpoint perspective on development. As you listen to this sample, note particularly the younger child's sound omissions and substitutions, but also that he displays rather mature, understandable sentences. Perhaps the most remarkable feature of the elementary-age child's speech development is how *similar* the speech of a kindergartner is to that of a sixth grader.

Benjie (age 4): I like the friend who has a dog that I played with.

Dad: Oh, yeah, he was a nice guy.

Andy (age 8): Who's he?

Dad: The fellow Benjie was playing with outside.

Andy: Oh, I didn't like him.

Dad: Oh, is that right? Why not?

Andy: Because he goes around bothering everybody . . . And he also does bad things in school and he's in third grade.

Dad: He's in third grade?

Andy: Yeah, like he doesn't study, and he talks all the time, and all that.

Dad: Yeah.

Benjie: I like him.

Dad: Yeah, well he's your friend, isn't he, Benjie?

Benjie: Andy, don't callin' him "Dummy."

Dad: Oh, I don't think Andy was calling him "Dummy," was he?

Benjie: He . . . he was.

Andy: Well that was cause he kicked his own dog. It was a pretty one, too.

Dad: Well, I don't think he should kick his dog, but I don't think you should call him "Dummy," either.

Andy: I never called him a "Dummy."

Dad: Okay.

Benjie: Yes, yes you did, Andy.

Andy: Oh, I did not.

Benjie: Oh yes you did.

TEACHING EFFECTIVE COMMUNICATION TO ELEMENTARY SCHOOLCHILDREN

The foregoing discussion implies an active, bustling, rather democratic home and classroom environment in which children share messages that can make a difference in the spheres they care about. Very little teaching of actual communication *concepts* is necessary or even desirable at the elementary level. Practice in sending and interpreting messages is what the child needs most.

Some parents and teachers are concerned that unless they *teach* specific grammar and communication etiquette concepts and *drill* children in their use the children are less likely to learn those concepts. This is only true to the extent that if children are allowed to participate more in their own development they will talk more like their parents or teachers *actually* talk than like their teachers *say they should* talk. The important point is more basic: The child is for all practical purposes a biologically programmed "language learning machine." Instruction in grammar is superfluous to his understandable speaking. To speak and listen effectively the child needs training in the forms of practice and meaningful communicative participation.

Further, communication development processes are tied closely to the child's genetic endowment; they can't be speeded up significantly by pushy parents or teachers.

You may ask: If it's all biological then why are parents and teachers needed at all? One reason is that even genetically determined behaviors can be affected—by bad environments. Baby ducks, for example, instinctively walk after their mothers, single file, soon after they are hatched. But if no mother appears and something else walks by the duck will follow it, become attached to it, and be uninterested in its mother later. If nothing walks by until the duck is half grown it will never follow or form attachments with anything.

Children's speech is somewhat similar to the baby duck—it needs a supportive, talk-centered environment to develop best. We all know about the worst kinds of environments—parental hostility, child beating, leaving children alone for long periods. Such environments likely will have unfortunate effects on speech. Less obvious but also harmful are the effects of adult correction of children's speech. Many adults, especially many teachers, have developed a reflex habit of "correcting" *everything* about children's speech that does not seem totally proper. The following utterances would be particularly liable to correction:

> You was at my house yesterday.
> I have three pencil.
> I don't have no cupcake.
> Can I have the crayon?
> I runned all the way here.

The correction comes immediately after the child's utterance and emphasizes the word with the "error." It is in much the same tone of voice one uses to speak to a pet:

> You *were* at my house yesterday.
> I have three pencil*s*.
> I don't have *any* cupcake.
> Do you mean *may* I have a crayon?
> I *ran* all the way home.

From a psychological perspective, these exchanges are degrading to the child. They emphasize his incompetence and liabilities for correction. Would your correct your friends so bluntly? Of course not—the tone is reserved for children, pets, and the incompetent.

From the perspective of learning, let's consider these correction exchanges as teaching devices. Correction puts a "correct" form close in time to the "incorrect" form. Seemingly, this assumes that the next time the form is used the learner will remember the correction and do it "right." Is it effective? Not in most cases, because it is basically *punishment*; and it punishes not only the particular item corrected but the entire utterance. The child speaking is trying to get a meaning across and to receive a meaningful response. When we correct his speech, he receives no meaningful response to his message. Therefore, he is less likely to speak again. Correction leads to quiet, angry children. In effect *they* say:

"Me love you."

and *we* respond:

"*I* love you."

They say:

"Killing cats are fun."

and we respond:

"Killing cats *is* fun."

In desperation, they mumble:

"School is so super far-out, dead-last boring."

And we respond:

"Johnny, speak up and please avoid slang in the classroom."

They remain silent.

Think about how much goes into a sentence—a meaningful thought or two and perhaps 50 sounds combined in phrases and sentences according to complex linguistic rules. To say a sentence a child must execute perhaps 100 tasks. If she does only one "wrong," are we likely to concentrate on that rather than on the 99 percent performed correctly?

Watch yourself—see how often you correct children's speech. We think you'll be surprised if you count all the corrections you make in one day and realize that most of them represent negative learning events for the children. We were somewhat appalled when we counted our own corrections. It is a thoroughly ingrained cultural pattern.

Does this mean you should totally *ignore* children's errors? No—the children's speech errors are important. There may be items that should be changed. Make a note of these. Use the correct forms yourself in conversation with children. You may be surprised at how fast they pick them up. The thing to avoid is bludgeoning children, however politely, with their incompetence.

Further, you can use children's errors to diagnose development. Many errors are good news. Such overgeneralizations as "runned," "goed," and so on show that the child has mastered regular verb forms. These do not need correction; the child will correct them on his own.

Finally, having listened to the child's speech for errors, you will know how to aid him on that rare circumstance when he directly *asks* for correction. In those cases and those cases *only* can correction be effective in communication instruction.

Our overall advice is to listen to children's speech with respect. Converse with children as if they were what they are—people. Think of children as guests in your classroom or home. Accept speech that is intelligible, meaningful, and moral from children as you would from a dinner guest. Since children learn to communicate by communicating, your being a moral, thinking, eloquent conversation partner is the best communication training possible. Have faith that nature's developmental processes will take care of children's language. You teach children to communicate effectively by doing so yourself when you are with them.

SUGGESTED ACTIVITIES

1. Listen to the speech samples for this chapter once again. As you listen, close your eyes, and try to "see" the whole situation—the room, how close people are to each other, the age of the parties, who seems to dominate, the general mood. These situational factors seem to be the most important variables affecting how a child (or adult) talks and sounds.

2. Listen to the samples that depict parents talking with their children. Ask yourself what kind of parent utterances seem to produce the most involvement and talking by children.

3. Try to transcribe the first and last taped segments of this chapter and count instances at each age level in which the child produces a sound markedly different from what an adult would make. In which instance(s) do you think these interferences might hinder effective communication?

4. If you taught first grade what could you do to be of maximum benefit to the child's developing communication skills? Why do you think this would be of benefit? How could you test your hypothesis?

Language Variation

3

Anyhow, they . . uh . . they got over there, the bus stopped to pick up all the other kids and it got . . . all the other kids got on the bus. Well, the mother was talking to this friend of hers or whatever and didn't notice that this little girl had hid in the back of the truck; she wasn't going to get on the bus. So . . uh . . . a few minutes these girls . . . my girls . . my . . uh . . students were telling me, a few minutes later this truck comes up behind the bus and starts flashing its lights and everything and so . . uh . . The bus driver pulled over and sure enough it was . . . it was Janie's mother bringing Janie to put her on the bus. And . . uh . . they said that it got to the point where every morning instead of just puttin' Janie on the bus like that and or anything like that, that one of the girls that was on the bus would get off and go down there and . . and you know, take her and pick her . . . well, pick her up or carry her or whatever into the bus and so that way she'd go, you know, and she'd sit there and talk to them or laugh with them or whatever, and this is how they got her to go to school. And, uh . . but I guess she made the adjustment all right after a . . . after a while . . uh, but this is the story that . . . that they told me. And I thought it was really cute, this little kindergarten girl already trying to play hooky.

DIALECTS AND "GOOD" ENGLISH

The following anecdote was told by Mrs. J., a teacher in east Texas. When the author commented that her speech was particularly interesting

45

because it contained many features characteristic of the English dialect spoken in east Texas, Mrs. J. indignantly replied that what she spoke was *not* a dialect; it was *good* English. Mrs. J., as do many people, assumed that the word "dialect" implied a negative judgment of her speech, a judgment that a linguist certainly would not intend to convey.

Mrs. J's strong reaction to the word "dialect" is not at all uncommon, and misunderstandings resulting from the linquists' use of that word dialect are not unusual. Thus, it is important to clarify exactly how the term "dialect" typically is used by linguists and others involved in the study of language, and consequently, how it will be used in this chapter.

Many people assume that dialect refers to bad, uncultured, or incorrect speech. Mrs. J. made that assumption in drawing a contrast between dialect and good English. Viewed in this way, a dialect is a corrupted form of some standard language, and people who speak dialects do not correctly speak the standard language. As far as Mrs. J. is concerned (and she is not alone), people may be divided into two major groups: people whose speech sounds like hers—the speakers of "good, correct English," and people whose speech sounds different from hers—those who speak a dialect. In other words, dialect as it usually is used and understood, is a pejorative term indicating the inadequacy or inappropriateness of another person's speech.

Linguists and others who study language use dialect in quite a different way. For them, it is not a term that involves any value judgment; that is, a dialect is neither good or bad. The word is a purely descriptive term that refers to language variation. Thus, if a linguist tells you that you speak a certain dialect, he or she is not in any way criticizing your speech. Rather, he is describing certain features of your speech that mark it as different—*not* better or worse—from the speech of other people. For the linguist, everyone speaks a dialect of a given language and that includes the linguist, too. To the linguist, then, the word "dialect" simply refers to the variations in how a language is spoken. The variation is in itself neither bad or good; it is simply a variation.

To understand the word "dialect" better, contrast it with two other words—*language* and *idiolect*. An idiolect, as the word itself indicates, is the idiosyncratic way an individual speaks. When you speak you use certain sounds, certain words, certain phrases, and certain kinds of sentences that are different from the sounds, words, phrases, and sentences used by other people—even by people who are very close to you. In our everyday lives we regularly recognize the idiosyncrasies that characterize human speech. You undoubtedly can identify many telephone callers by certain aspects of their speech that you have come to recognize even before they identify themselves. You hear the voice of a well-known person, e.g., a politician, on the radio and recognize him or her without the name being announced. Your own speech is regularly recognized by people who know you; there is something special about your speech that makes it different from everyone else's. Each person has an individual way of speaking, and this individualized speech is what linguists call an *idiolect.* Speech is so idiosyncratic, in fact, that voiceprints now are sometimes used instead of fingerprints to identify people.

A broader term than idiolect, dialect refers to the speech of a group of speakers called a *speech community.* In its broadest sense, a speech community is any group of two or more individuals who interact verbally and whose speech reflects some common features, however these features may be defined. Thus, a speech community may be a family group, a neighborhood, a city, a county, a state, a region, or even a whole country. For example, we can speak of the American English dialect community in contrast to the British English dialect community. Another way of viewing a speech community is in terms of specific occupations or life styles. For example, attorneys have certain ways of speaking in the courtroom, and all attorneys may be considered in this sense to belong to a single speech community. The same thing may be said for musicians, physicians, teachers, and football coaches. There are certain features that characterize the speech of the members of these groups; and consequently, they may be considered speech communities with special, identifiable, dialect features.

The third term we mentioned above was *language.* The traditional distinction between dialect and language is that two different dialects usually are mutually intelligible and that two different languages are not. That is, the speakers of two dialects of the same language usually can understand each other with a minimum of difficulty, but speakers of two different languages usually cannot understand each other. For example, speakers of two principal dialects of English—American and British—usually understand each other reasonably well even though they do notice the obvious differences in their dialects. Of course, the distinction between language and dialect is not absolutely clear-cut. There are speakers of American English who find certain British dialects almost unintelligible. On the other hand, when speakers of two different languages come into contact with each other it is almost inevitable that they will ultimately influence each other so that words and expressions from one language may be incorporated into the other. When speakers of two different languages co-exist in close proximity for a long period of time (e.g., along the United States-Mexico border), linguistic borrowings are common. It is not at all unusual to hear such utterances as, "Her leg . . . no mas estaba asi . . . sticking out," where the two languages—English and Spanish—are used in the same sentence. Sometimes new dialects (*pidgins*) and new languages (*creoles*) develop from this regular contact between speakers of two different languages. In spite of the lack of an absolutely clear-cut distinction between the terms *language* and *dialect,* the contrast is nonetheless useful when discussing human speech.

Language variation may be considered from at least three distinct perspectives, and the remainder of this chapter will be devoted to discussing them. The first is the *geographical perspective* in which speech variation is viewed as distributed across a map. People from one region speak differently from people from another region. Language variations thus considered are, not surprisingly, called *regional* or *geographical dialects.*

A second perspective is social; within a given geographical area people from different socially identifiable groups speak differently. In your everyday dealings with different kinds of businessmen, co-workers, friends, and relatives, you have probably noticed that although they all reside and work in the same geographical region, their speech may differ in terms of the words and expressions they use, the kinds of sentences they employ, and even the sounds within those sentences. As you already have undoubtedly guessed, these variations viewed from a social perspective are called social dialects or *sociolects.*

The third and last perspective we will consider involves the variations that occur as a function of the social situation in which speakers find themselves at a given moment in time. You probably have noticed in your own speech that there are times when you attempt to speak more formally—for example, when being interviewed for a job or trying to impress your listener. There are other times when your speech is quite informal—for example, when you are enjoying a relaxed conversation with good friends. This variation, which is socially codified in a speech community, is called *register switching* or *stylistic variation.*

In the following sections we will provide speech samples to illustrate the variations in language just described. To get a true feeling for these variations, you will need to listen to the recording of these samples.

REGIONAL DIALECTS

Do you think that somebody out in the West would talk any differently than you would?

Allison: Yeah.

Why do you suppose that is?

Because they live in a different place.

Yeah. Just because they live in a different place they talk differently, I guess, huh?

Yeah.

Which part of the country do you think has the most unusual type of speaking?

Well, . . . maybe Japan.

Yeah. How about . . . which part of the United States has the most interesting pa . . . interesting type of speaking?

Uh . . . Texas.

Yeah?

Yeah.

What parts of the country have you been to?

Well, I've been to Florida, and I've been to . . . Vermont, and I've been to North Carolina . . .

What do you want to do when you get out of school . . . when you're no longer going to school?

I want to be a TV repairlady.

A TV repairlady . . . that's a pretty good idea.

Yeah.

Why is that?

Well, because you get to work with little things in the TV, and . . uh . . also you probably get lots of TVs for free.

If you had heard Allison, a nine-year-old fourth grader, you would probably have guessed that she was from New York. Next is Ellen, also nine and a fourth grader, from Houston, Texas, who is talking with her older sister, Sally.

Sally: Tell me what Clara has been doing, Ellen.

Ellen: Oh . . . she's been in the hospital a lot. She's just . . . she's been real sick . . . and she . . . um . . . worms . . . heart worms.

What kind of dog is she?

A basset.

Mmm . . well, that's too bad. Is she taking some kind of medicine or anything?

Oh yes . . . she has to take this whole . . . a great big bottle. And . . . uh . . she has to take a teaspoon a day. And I don't . . . it's kind of weird . . . I hope Jim feeds her out of a old spoon.

Why? Does he put a spoon in her mouth?

Uh huh.

I'll bet its's the one you have in your cereal every morning.

Sally . . . gosh, that's mean.

If you had heard Ellen, you wouldn't have had much trouble recognizing her Texas dialect. The fact that the written versions of Allison's and Ellen's speech don't show any major differences illustrates the point that New York and Texas accents differ mainly in speech sounds. There are also some differences in grammar and vocabulary, but these do not often show up in brief speech samples.

The differences between the speech of Allison and of Ellen may be attributed to the fact that they have lived in two distinct dialect regions of the United States. Allison was born in the New York area where both of her parents were born and grew up. Ellen, on the other hand, was born in Texas where her parents grew up. If you listen to the recording, what specific differences do you notice in the speech of these two children?

Since we claim that people who grow up and live in the same geographical region share certain dialect features, and since both Allison and her father (with whom she is talking in the sample) grew up in New York, there should be similarities between Allison's and her father's speech. Can you hear these similarities? What about Ellen and her sister, Sally, who grew up in the same area—are there similarities in the way they speak?

Ellen and Allison, like all children, began speaking in the home environment. From the earliest stage of their speech development, they heard a dialect—the dialect spoken by their parents and other relatives. The English (or any other language) a child learns is not dialect free; the child's parents and others in the environment all speak a dialect to which the child regularly is exposed. For Allison and Ellen, most of the people who surrounded them as they began talking—parents, relatives, and friends—spoke a specific regional dialect (New York or Texas) that helped shape the way Allison and Ellen now speak.

The speech of children from two other regions of the United States may help to illustrate the diversity of regional dialects. Again, to sense the similarities and differences in their speech and in the speech of Allison and Ellen whom you heard earlier, listen to the recording.

Carol is nine years old and lives in Maryland.

You have pierced ears. Why don't you tell me how you got your ears pierced.

Carol: Well, last year I wanted to get my ears pierced and my mother said that if I still wanted them when I was nine I could get 'em pierced. So, one day we went to the doctor's, and he just put this stuff on a needle and on my ears and stuck the needles in my ears with a shot. Then he made holes for the earrings and then . . . he just stuck the earrings in.

Did he tell you to go home and do something special to your ears?

Yeah. He told me to put alcohol on 'em every day and sleep with my earrings in . . . these . . . I'm wearing.

Do you like to have your ears pierced?

It's fun . . . unless like . . . like one day I hit it . . . my ear with my shoe and it got all swollen.

David is seven and from California.

> Do you have any pets?
> *David:* I used to have a mouse and we still have a rat.
> Well, what happened to your mouse?
> Oh, it ran away.
> It ran away?
> Yeah.
> Tell me about your rat.
> Uh . . we found him in the sewer . . . we found him in the gutter . . . and we have . . . we have different kind of gutters. And he was down and our nextdoor neighbor, Mr. Morrison, opened it up and opened it up and got the rat out.
> And gave it to you, uh?
> Yeah. And gave it to us.
> What are some other kind of things you have to do for a rat?
> You have to clean his cage and feed him and . . and . . uh . . give him a drink.*

Gradually, as children mature, other influences begin to play a role in shaping their speech. They begin interacting with other children, first in the immediate neighborhood and then in school. Children spend considerable time talking with each other, and the influence of one child's speech on that of another should not be underestimated. Later, children encounter members of a broader speech community—some of whom speak in much the same manner they do and others who sound "different" or, as some children put it, "funny." For example, if Ellen were to listen to the following recordings of two United States presidents whose dialects were well known, which one would sound more "natural" to her? Which one might sound "funny?" Do you think Allison would have the same reaction? Why?

> *John F. Kennedy:* I'm not satisfied until every American enjoys his full constitutional rights. If a Negro baby is born (and this is true also of Puerto Ricans and Mexicans) in some of our cities, he has about one-half as much chance to get through high school as a white baby. He has one-third as much chance to get through college as a white student. He has about a third as much chance to be a professional man; about half as much chance to own a house. He has about four times as much chance that he'll be out of work in his life as the white baby. I think we can do better. I don't want the talents of any American to go to waste.

> *Lyndon B. Johnson:* The issue of equal rights for American Negroes *is* such an issue. And, should we defeat every enemy, and should we double our wealth and conquer the stars, and still be unequal to *this* issue, then we will have failed as a people and as a nation.

All of us begin to learn to discriminate between speakers who sound like us and speakers who sound different from us; by the time we are adults

*David may be heard on tape in Chapter 6.

we recognize certain features of regional dialects when we hear them. These differences, the identifying characteristics of regional dialects, are acquired unconsciously. Children are not aware that they learn certain features of speech typical of the region in which they live, and parents are not aware that they "teach" them. These regional dialect features appear in children's speech simply because they are present in the environment as they learn to talk. Just as none of us probably would state categorically that one region of the United States is absolutely better than another (though we may have preferences as to climate, scenery, social life, and so on), it is equally foolish to speak of one regional dialect as being "better than" or "superior to" another. Regional dialects characterize regions; regions differ, and regional dialects differ.

Although we have concentrated on dialects of American English, it should be obvious that there are regional variations in all languages. In Spanish, for example, the Puerto Rican dialect contains features that do not occur in the dialect spoken in Mexico. Just as we English speakers learn to associate certain features of speech with certain regions of the United States, Spanish speakers also recognize certain features in the Spanish of Cubans, Puerto Ricans, or Mexicans, which are typical of those regions of the Spanish-speaking world (See Chapter 5). All languages spoken over an extended geographical area show the kind of regional dialect variations we have described.

In closing this discussion of regional dialects, let's consider briefly how different regional dialects develop. In very simple terms, we can say they develop because members of a given group of people speak to each other more than they speak to members of another group of people; and this process has continued throughout the history of man. For example, people who live in Texas speak to other Texans more often than they speak to people who live in Ohio; and Ohioans speak to other Ohioans more frequently than they speak to people who live in Idaho. A sound, a word, or an expression that may be very common in Virginia might be unknown to someone from Massachusetts who never has heard it uttered. Part of the reason for these differences is that the people who settled in Virginia and Massachusetts were from different regions of England, and these regions of England were themselves characterized by different dialects. In the past, before advances in transportation and communication made contacts possible, dialects developed on a regional basis over a period of time because speakers living in widely diverse regions had little or no opportunity to communicate with each other. Such natural barriers to communication and transportation as mountain ranges and deserts often served to separate one group of speakers from another, and this isolation allowed the languages of the two isolated groups to evolve gradually and independently.

This gradual evolution of different dialects may be exemplified by examining Spanish, Portuguese, and French. At one time what are now separate languages were dialects of the same language—Latin. When the

Roman soldiers went to the far reaches of the empire, they took with them their dialect—usually referred to as Vulgar Latin, or the Latin spoken by the average Roman. Vulgar Latin was carried to what is now modern Spain, Portugal, and France. In each of these three regions it evolved independently for some time. This evolution resulted in what we now would describe as three dialects of Vulgar Latin—one spoken in Spain, another in Portugal, and the third in France. The speakers of one dialect still were able to understand the speakers of the others, but they noticed that speakers from the other dialect areas did not sound quite the same as they did. After more time elapsed, the dialects of Vulgar Latin had evolved further, and speakers of one dialect no longer readily understood speakers of the others. At this point, the three dialects took on the status of the three separate languages they are today. Since the process is evolutionary, it is not possible to state at what precise time the three dialects became distinct languages, just as it is not possible in many geographical regions to locate the precise boundary between two dialects or languages.

Regional dialects, then, are generally the result of two principal factors: (1) the settlement history of a region, i.e., where the people who settled there came from; and (2) the communication networks between people in the region and those in surrounding areas. If communication between two regions is frequent, similarities in speech may be expected to occur; if communication is infrequent or nonexistent, similarities in speech patterns will be less likely. Within the same region people who engage in the same or similar activities will tend to communicate with each other more frequently than those who engage in different activities. This frequency of communication leads to similarities in the way people speak. When people from the same geographical region differ in terms of educational background or occupation, their speech also may differ. These variations, characterizing social dialects, will be dealt with in the following section.

SOCIAL DIALECTS

People from the same geographical region do not all sound alike. In fact, they may exhibit considerable variation in the way they speak—using different sounds, words, expressions, and sentence patterns. Often these speech differences within a single community are found to correlate with such social variables as education, occupation, and the resulting social status within the community. Speech variants used by socially identifiable groups of speakers are known as social dialects or sociolects.

Social dialects are typically divided into two broad categories: standard and nonstandard dialects. Speakers of a standard dialect are typically well educated and have occupations that place them at a middle or high socioeconomic level. Standard dialect speakers are often geographically mobile (living in different places and traveling to still others). They maintain their contact with the standard dialect by reading and listening to nationally disseminated materials and by interacting with other standard dialect speakers in occupational and social settings. Speakers of a nonstandard dialect are usually people who have had a limited education. They often remain in one geographical location, and their speech contacts are primarily with others of the same kind of background.

A very important point about the standard versus nonstandard dialect distinction is that the standard is not determined by any absolute authority. That is, there is no official agency or individual who determines that certain ways of speaking are acceptable (standard) and certain others are not (nonstandard). Who, then, determines what is standard speech? Well, it is the speakers themselves who ultimately determine what is acceptable and what is not; and like fashions in clothing or music, these acceptable features change from time to time. What was unacceptable years ago may now be a common feature of the standard dialect. For example, although it used to be important in educated speech to make a distinction between *shall* and *will,* nowadays there are probably very few standard dialect speakers who conscientiously make this distinction. In addition, new words and expressions or new meanings for old words and expressions regularly appear and are accepted into the standard dialect. If standard dialect speakers regularly use a given word—say, *hopefully, inoperative,* or even *ain't*—that word becomes part of the standard dialect. Occasionally protests are registered against changes in the language (e.g., the furor over Webster's Third International Dictionary) by people who think they must defend language standards from the abuses of the speakers of the language, but acceptability necessarily resides with those who actually use the language. They are the only ones who can set a standard.

Children, too, reflect either a standard or nonstandard dialect in their speech. Obviously, the dialect they speak is not the result of their formal educational background or their occupation. The child matures in a language learning environment that reflects the social dialect spoken by his or her parents, relatives, neighbors, and friends. Children whose parents and friends speak a nonstandard dialect typically will speak a nonstandard dialect, and children who are surrounded by standard dialect speakers will tend to speak a more standard dialect. Consider now Brian, a six-year-old who speaks a standard dialect of English.

> I want you to tell me what starts fights around here.
> *Brian:* Doug, mostly.
> Mostly Doug. How does that happen?
> Well, it starts mean . . . it starts with mean talk.

> Mean talk. What kind of thing would be mean talk? Could you give me an example?

Well, an example would maybe get in a fight. "Quit it, Doug . . . Will you stop it?"

Mm hmm . . . Is that . . . that's the kind of talk that you would do after the fight started, usually, hmm? Or is this before the fight you're talking about?

Well, this . . um . . happens . . um . . when Doug does something like hit me.

Oh, I see. Does it happen sometimes when he's playing with a toy and you wish he wasn't? . . . when you say, "Quit it?"

Well, no . . . it does happen when he's playing with a toy he's not supposed to.

I see. Well, how can you tell if it's a toy he's not supposed to?

Well, if it's new.

If it's new, then he's not supposed to.

Yeah. Like if Doug got my library card and did something with it . . . he shouldn't've . . . I should stop him before he does anything.

But, after your library card is older it would be Okay?

No. But that's *one* thing that's not allowed to get touched.

Compare Brian with Harold, who is nine. Harold's speech contains nonstandard dialect features not found in Brian's speech. Brian and Harold thus may be said to speak different social dialects of English. In addition to the social dialect differences that distinguish Harold's speech from Brian's, there are also obvious regional differences. Harold grew up in Kentucky and Brian in Wisconsin. This dual set of dialect differences—social and regional—in the boys' speech illustrates the important fact that everybody's speech contains both regional and social dialect features.

Hi, Aunt Grace. This is Harold. Come over one of these days and bring Uncle Al and Richard, and Richard and me and Darrel can go fishing, hunting, and frog-gigging. And we can play croquet, ride bikes, do a lot of stuff. I'm going to sing a song for ya.

You get a line, I'll get a pole, honey.
You get a line, I'll get a pole, babe.
You get a line, I'll get a pole,
We'll go fishing in the crawdad hole,
Honey, baby mine.

It is important to emphasize that children who speak a nonstandard dialect are not limited to speaking that dialect for the rest of their lives. One of the important effects of education is that it introduces the standard

dialect. And it is equally important to emphasize that when children are exposed to and learn the standard dialect in school—be they Chicano children learning a standard dialect of Spanish or black children learning a standard dialect of English—it is not necessarily at the expense of the nonstandard dialect they may bring with them. Most children who enter school speaking a nonstandard dialect learn the standard dialect as a second and alternative dialect, and they become able throughout the rest of their lives to shift from one dialect to the other when the situation calls for it.

Nonstandard dialect speakers who acquire a standard second dialect are not the only ones who vary their speech according to the situation. Psychologists talking with other psychologists use certain terms that are technical in nature and that carry a very precise meaning for them. They may not use these terms when talking to nonpsychologists, and if they do use them it will be in a less technical way. The same can be siad for engineers, musicians, carpenters, teachers, and circus performers. The label applied to these terms used in conjunction with a specific profession or life style is *jargon*; almost every endeavor—from skydiving to bookkeeping—has a special terminology or technical jargon connected with it. Another source of variation occurs when members of a group speak in a special way that identifies membership in the group and that is designed deliberately to exclude outsiders. The term applied to this group-speech is *slang*. A group of prisoners, for example, may develop special ways of talking so as to exclude such outsiders as guards. Young people, too, often develop slang words and expressions that are used to exclude adults or other outsiders from understanding what they are talking about. Often, they use their slang expressions with members of their group of friends and speak differently when talking with adults. It is important to note that because slang expressions often involve a deliberate attempt to avoid being understood, they usually have a short life span. As they become more widely used (e.g., on the evening news) outsiders begin to understand and use them, and new slang expressions must be invented or new meanings assigned to old expressions so that outsiders once again are excluded.

STYLISTIC VARIATION

In addition to speech variations resulting from regional and social influences, most of us, including young children, regularly vary our speech to suit the occasion and the person(s) with whom we are interacting. With friends in an informal setting (e.g., at home), we typically use an informal, familiar style; an encounter with these same friends in a more formal setting (e.g., at a meeting) would probably result in a more formal speech style. With superiors or strangers in less familiar settings, the more formal, cautious speech style typically is employed. Consider now Ellen, the little girl from

Texas whom we heard earlier, as she talks with her older sister, Sally, about airplane travel. In the first conversation Ellen and Sally are alone, and Ellen's speech is very informal. In the second conversation Ellen and Sally are joined by their father, and Ellen seems less relaxed, more formal in her speech. As you listen to the recording, make a note of the specific aspects of Ellen's speech that differ from one conversation to the next. Do you notice any difference in the way Sally speaks when her father is present? What reasons can you think of for the marked difference between these two conversations?

> *Sally:* I'll bet you're excited about going to Tulsa.
>
> *Ellen:* Oh, yeah. I can't wait to see Amy and Suzy and Uncle James and Nancy.
>
> Well, tell me what you're all going to do and everything.
>
> Oh, we get . . . I get to go with Suzy to lifeguard and swim and everything.
>
> Well, great. Are y'all going to fly or drive?
>
> Fly.
>
> Do you like to?
>
> Yeah.
>
> Tell me what your . . . tell me about your trips that you've had in planes before. What's your favorite part and all that kind of stuff.
>
> My favorite part is when we take off and land.
>
> Oh, well that's good. Do you . . . do your ears ever pop?
>
> Nope . . . only the first time.
>
> Oh, I see. Well, do you chew gum to prevent it and that kind of stuff?
>
> Well, I usually don't chew gum, but that time I did.
>
> Do you ever get a mixed drink or anything on the plane?
>
> Noooooooooooo!
>
> Do you think Eddie will?
>
> No. She just gets a Coke or something.
>
> Well that sounds better anyway.

This informal conversation may be contrasted with Ellen and Sally's discussion of a similar topic when their father is present.

> *Father:* Do you ever look out of the window of the airplane, Ellen, when . . uh . . you can see the ground and . . . and . . .
>
> *Ellen:* Yes, sir.

. . . look at the rivers and . . .

Yes, sir.

Sally: What different things do you see on the ground?

Oh, just houses, and cars and . . . I don't know . . . just a whole bunch of stuff.

What color does it look like mostly when you look down? What color is the predominant one? The . . .

Blue.

Blue . . . for water? You think that is?

Mm hmm.

Or it could be just the blue haze . . . it's a general haze over the landscape . . .

Yeah. Do you see a lot of interesting people . . .

Mm hmm.

. . . when you fly?

Mm hmm.

Have you ever seen anyone that was what you might be called a personality on the plane?

No, sir.

. . . anyone who was famous?

No, sir.

Who is the most famous person you have ever seen?

I haven't seen anybody.

As Ellen spoke with her sister and father, she probably was not aware of the changes she made in her speech. Like Ellen, most of us switch back and forth from one speech style to another without any awareness that we are doing it. It is almost as though we have an automatic sensor that evaluates the listener and the setting and adjusts our speech style accordingly. For example, a teacher may speak one way to her pupils in class—"All right, children, let's go"—and quite another way to her own children at home—"Will you kids come on?" The master of ceremonies at a large public gathering may attempt to quiet the crowd by repeatedly but politely requesting, "May I have your attention, please?" The same individual will attempt to quiet his children with, "Will you shut up!"

These style shifts are so well codified socially in the speech community, and we have all become so accustomed to them, that we are able to recognize easily the incongruity between speech style and a given situation. The players in a huddle would no doubt wonder about a player who responded to the question, "Who's gonna carry the ball"? with: "Well, after giving this matter considerable thought, I should like to suggest that the most appropriate

utilization of our human resources would involve the selection of our most competent and consistently successful performer to represent us in the forthcoming confrontation with the opposition—namely, yours truly." Because the speech style is inappropriate to the setting and the listeners, we find the result ludicrous.

An incongruous style also may be used deliberately to provide the listener with an additional "message." A father who finds the beat-up old car of one of his son's friends blocking his driveway as he attempts to hurry out to the airport to catch a plane may say to the boy, "Will you be so kind as to move your limousine to a more appropriate location." His clenched teeth, red face, and deliberately formal speech style all serve to indicate the seriousness of his message.

The differences in style we have just discussed are obvious; the choice of words and syntactical patterns are clearly indicative of the speaker's intention. Other indications of style are more subtle, however, such as the use of contractions, e.g., *we'll* for *we will*, or *he's* for *he is* or *he has.* In very formal speech, contractions often are avoided, but in informal speech they regularly are used in place of the corresponding two-word constructions where the use of these two-word constructions would sound out of place and unduly formal to the listener. Another more subtle mark of style is the *-ing* ending on verbs. In some informal speech this ending is typically reduced to *-in'* as in, "He's goin.'" In formal speech this ending typically is pronounced in full. One study found that even small children used the full *-ing* ending in a more formal interview setting and reduced it to *-in'* when the situation became more informal. This is not to suggest, of course, that the children were consciously aware of their use of this verb ending. But it does suggest that from an early age speakers begin to become sensitive to speech style, and they unconsciously differentiate stylistic features in their own speech.

How do children come to know about these stylistic variations in speech? Well, most of them learn them from other people with whom they come in contact—parents, speakers on television, and from their teachers. In fact, one of the very important ways a teacher can contribute to his or her pupils' language development is to present examples of how speech may vary to suit the occasion. Children can learn that justified or not, people often are judged by the way they speak (see Chapter 6), and a job or a loan may be lost easily because the interviewer did not react favorably to the speech of the job or loan seeker.

One of the goals of our educational system should be to provide all children with a flexibility of speech styles that permits them to interact with a variety of persons in a variety of settings. It should be noted that the emphasis here is on developing a *flexibility* of speech styles, not on making everybody conform to some formal speech standard. Language development does not mean replacing a child's informal style with a more formal style. None of us speaks formally on all occasions, and it is unrealistic to expect or train children to do so. True language development involves the acquisition of a variety of speech styles appropriate to changing social contexts and ultimately, of the ability to switch automatically from one speech style to another as the speech setting changes.

FINAL NOTES

All three of the variations in language just mentioned—geographical, social, and stylistic—are present in the speech of a given individual at a given moment. When you open your mouth to speak, your utterance is governed by the geographical region where you grew up, your social status, and by the stylistic level you wish to employ at that moment. There is no way to avoid reflecting these factors in our speech; all are present whenever we speak. It can be said that the way we speak is very much the result of our past history—of where we learned to speak, from whom, and under what conditions.

This is not to suggest, however, that we cannot change the way we speak; we are not the mere victims of our own history. Your own language undoubtedly has undergone considerable changes during the past three or four years. You undoubtedly are using new words and expressions you did not use four years ago, and you are understanding words and expressions you did not know then. Throughout our lives our language continually is affected by the language that surrounds us. We hear new words and expressions and unconsciously incorporate them into our own speech. We gradually, and again unconsciously, stop using words and expressions that may have been very frequent in our past speech. One very important factor that affects language is, of course, school. Teachers can play a crucial role in providing students with linguistic alternatives (e.g., standard dialect and stylistic variations) and in shaping attitudes about language and speech. To ensure that the school's effect on a child's language development is positive, teachers and parents should be aware of the kind of considerations concerning language that have been discussed in this chapter.

SUGGESTED ACTIVITIES

1. Make a list of those features that you think specify the speech of the east Texas teacher as being from that geographical region. If you are from another geographical region, indicate how your own speech differs from hers.

2. Compare specific features of the speech samples of Ellen, Carol, and David. What are the major differences you notice in these samples?

Does one of the speakers stand out as significantly different from the other two? Which one?

3. Listen again to the east Texas teacher, Ellen, and to President Johnson. What similarities do you notice in these three speech samples?

4. You undoubtedly have relatives, friends, or acquaintances who come from different geographical regions. If possible, make a tape recording of samples of their speech. List features that characterize their speech as typical of a given geographical region.

5. If you are now teaching, consider the speech of the children in your class. Do any of these children come from different geographical regions? If possible, record short samples of the children's speech. Are there differences in the way they speak that you think result from their being from different geographical regions?

6. When you listen to or watch news programs, listen especially for the speech characteristics of persons in the news who represent different geographical regions (e.g., senators from different states). What regional dialect features occur in their speech?

7. Compare the speech of Brian and Harold with the speech samples found in Chapter 4. List features of these samples that in your opinion reflect social differences in speech.

8. Comedians and situation comedy programs on television often use regional and social differences in speech as a device to make us laugh. Can you think of examples of the exploitation of speech differences to create humor in the programs you watch? Describe the characters and the aspects of their speech that identify them.

9. Authors frequently attempt to characterize speech differences in dialogue that appears on the printed page. They will, for example, write "gonna" for "going to," "wuz" for "was," and "I dunno" for "I don't know." This technique often is referred to as *eye dialect,* that is, a dialect that we perceive visually. Can you find examples of this technique in works with which you are familiar? Why does an author do this? What is the desired effect on the reader?

10. For the pairs of expressions listed below, indicate social situations in which each expression would be appropriate and situations in which that same expression would be totally inappropriate.

     A. May I have your attention, please?
        Shut up and listen.

B. No way I'm gonna do that.
   I'd rather not do that.

C. Don't bug me.
   Can we discuss it later?

D. I have reason to question the veracity of your statement.
   That's a lie.

E. Shall we go?
   Let's get out of here.

F. I beg your pardon?
   Huh?

G. He's a fool.
   I sometimes wonder whether he is able to distinguish between reality and fantasy.

H. Bye-bye.
   Good-bye.

I. That's what you think!
   I'm afraid I must disagree with you on this matter.

J. Hey man, what's happening?
   It's nice to see you again.

K. What do you want?
   May I help you?

L. It's none of your business.
   I'm sorry, I'd rather not discuss it.

M. Excuse me, please.
   Get out of the way.

N. One moment, please.
   Just a second.

The Sounds of Black English

4

WHAT IS BLACK ENGLISH?

Many teachers have observed that the speech of some black children tends to "sound different" from that of most white children in fairly consistent ways. Systematic differences between any two varieties of speaking within a language can be described as dialect differences, as we discussed in Chapter 3. It seems reasonable to state that some black children speak different *dialects,* just as children from Boston and from Georgia speak different dialects. Consider this speech sample from a fourth grader named Eldridge.

> Now, uh, could you tell me something about the TV shows you watch? What kind of shows do you watch?
>
> *Eldridge:* I don't watch the TV.
>
> You don't watch the TV?
>
> No, sir.
>
> Well, my goodness, tell me why. Why not?
>
> I'm saved.
>
> You're saved?
>
> Uh huh.

67

Well what does that mean?

It means, you see, see, see you're saved, God save you and fill you with the Holy Gos, and you don't pose' to watch TV, cause that's in the worl.

Oh, now that's interesting, that's interesting. Tell me about you getting saved, will you?

See, when you firs get saved you repent of your sins and tell the Lord forgive you all what you doin. Then, and then you speaking in tongues and you don't know what you be saying, you filled with the Holy Ghost and you don't do, you don't smoke like you used to and you don't drink and do all that.

All right, go ahead.

And um, and you don't wear . . . you don't wear long curls, cause the Bible say it's a shame for men to have long curl. You don't drink, smoke, and take dope and all that. That's all.

Well, fine, fine, sounds great! Tell me now, what led up to your being saved?

See, we went to this church on Ford and my mother got saved and she told us about it, so we got saved.

Well, well, well, how do you go about getting saved?

See, you go to the church and the Pastor, he be preaching, and then when he call the line you go right up and he'll ask you what do you want God to do for you, and then when you say save, he'll tell you, "Lift your hands to the Lord," and until then, then you get saved and He'll forgive all your sins. And then you get saved.

Is that right?

Yes, sir.

Un huh. Can you tell me how you felt when you got saved?

See, I felt a new person, I felt different. You feel different, you feel clean.

Is that right?
Yes, sir.
How long have you been saved?
About three years.
Now you spoke of your mother, uh when we started talking about being saved? Uh, could you tell me something about her, and do you have sisters and brothers?
Yes, sir.
Could you tell me about them, just a little something about them?
Well my sisters, they used to wear those short dresses, miniskirts and pants, when they got saved, they don't wear them no more. They don't wear miniskirts and pants no more. My mother, she don't cuss like

like she used to cuss and smoke and fuss, see she just, she's saved and
she act a new person.

Um hum.

And my brother, from then on, don't be fighting no more, don't be
fighting no more, we used to fight a lot of times. We used to fight a lot
of times, we don't fight no more, we act saved and we nice, but we
don't fuss and do all that, and be with the world, or bell bottoms and
all them, we don't wear than.

Um hum, um hum, well, now that is interesting. Now did you tell me
anything about your father, I can't remember?

Well he's out of town somewhere, he's not saved.

He's not . . .

Eldridge's speech represents "Black English" as this dialect has been
described by Ralph Fasold and Walt Wolfram of the Center for Applied
Linguistics. His speech is distinctive in several aspects of pronunciation
and grammar.

Pronunciation.   Several slightly unusual pronunications occue in
Black English. "R" and "l" sounds are sometimes weak or absent: "carrot"
becomes "cat." "Th" sounds often become "t" or "d": "the" becomes
"de," "throw" becomes "trow." Also, some southernisms persist in
Black English, even among northerners: "pen" is pronounced "pin,"
"time" becomes "tahm (Tom)". Such differences cause a few homonyms
that are unique to Black English. One might expect such homonyms to
create considerable confusion, but they actually are a minor problem. All
dialects contain many homonyms; they are the source of puns. The context
of an utterance is usually sufficient to make a word's meaning clear in any
dialect.

The most important, and perhaps universal, sound feature in Black
English is simplification of consonant clusters at ends of words. In
Black English, when a word ends with two consonant sounds, the last
sound in the word is likely to be omitted.

"First" becomes "firs."
"World" becomes "worl."
"Expect" becomes "expec."
"Desk" becomes "des."

This problem causes frequent misunderstanding between Black English
speakers and their teachers. The problem is severe, because many grammatical
endings of English depend upon final consonants. For example, omitting the
last consonant of a cluster causes the following changes in pronunciation.

"Missed" becomes "miss."
"Saved" becomes "save."
"Walked" becomes "walk."

Such changes may lead teachers to think that a child does not know how to form the past tense.

Other misinterpretations can be caused by omitting a final "s."

"Tells" becomes "tell."
"Sings" becomes "sing."
"Curls" becomes "curl."

These omissions could make a teacher believe that the child cannot form third-person-singular verbs.

In forming possessives,

"Joe's pencil" becomes "Joe pencil."
"Fred's book" becomes "Fred book."

The above examples could lead a teacher to believe that the child cannot form possessives.

The omission of -s could persuade teachers that the child cannot form plurals.

"Trucks" becomes "truck."
"My sisters" becomes "my sister."

Like Eldridge, many Black English-speaking children can be expected to exhibit any of these forms sometimes. Teachers unfamiliar with Black English could conclude that these children are not learning important aspects of grammar.

Grammar. Some teachers feel that Black English is very distinctive in grammar. Actually, grammar differences between Black English and other dialects are quite small. Most supposed grammar differences are simply misinterpreted consonant cluster reductions as described above. Some of the real differences follow.

Black English employs some characteristic forms of the commonly used verb *to be.* Sometimes, the "be" particle is missing from present and future tense. Thus, Eldridge's "she's saved" sounds more like "She saved." Probably this is a reduced consonant at the end of a word and not a grammatical difference. Eldridge's use of correct past tense forms in

such other sentences as, "They got saved" indicates that he understands past tense.

In addition to tense differences with "to be," speakers of Black English sometimes employ a form of "be" that refers to a meaning that appears not to exist in other dialects of English. "He be sick," for example, means that he is sick a good deal of the time. Eldridge's, "The Pastor he be preaching," and "You don't know what you be saying," indicate conditions that are frequently repeated.

Black English speakers often use *pronomial apposition,* which refers to placing a pronoun near the noun to which it refers: "My dog, he runs fast." This usage, interestingly, is permissible in many English dialects, but only if there are other words in between. "My dog, the big one with brown spots, he runs fast." Eldridge's speech uses frequent pronomial apposition: "My sisters, they . . . ," and "My mother, she . . . "

Also, Black English speakers commonly use forms of *negation* that are used in White, nonstandard dialects but are unacceptable in White polite speech. Use of "ain't" is one example. The most important problem usage in this area and the one to which many teachers react most strongly is the *double negative:* "Nobody can't do that." Eldridge occasionally uses this construction, apparently for extra emphasis: "They don't wear them no more."

Some writers have claimed that double negatives are illogical—that speakers and listeners cannot be sure whether "You don't know nothing" means "You know nothing" or "You know something." The vast majority of such usages are clearly for added emphasis, not for negative negation. Further, many of the world's languages including French, Russian, Spanish, and Hungarian use double negatives as acceptable forms.

The above discussion illustrates linguistic differences that support the statement that some black children speak a dialect form that could be called "Black English" instead of dialects that many white children speak. But such a statement must be interpreted with at least four reservations.

First, as we mentioned in Chapter 3, there are many dialects of American English that spring from regional and social as well as ethnic differences among speakers. It is easier to identify a speech sample as sounding somehow representative of a given dialect than to describe how it sounds different. It is extremely difficult to predict whether regional, social, or ethnic dialect markings will dominate what a child's speech "sounds like."

Second, not all black people speak Black English. The features noted above as constituting Black English most commonly have been observed in the speech of northern, urban, black male, teenagers of working class status when talking to each other. Older and wealthier black Americans tend to sound more "standard." Some young children appear to speak Black English; others do not.

Third, Black English is linguistically more similar to standard English than different from it. We introduced the concept of Black English by demonstrating some linguistic descriptions of how black children "sound different" from white children. That discussion did not mention the fact that blacks and whites sound much more alike than different. Both speak American English; both can speak in sentences that can be understood by members of the other race. Eldridge's speech may sound definitely "Black" to you, but we wager you had little difficulty understanding his meanings. Furthermore, many features of Black English also occur in other dialects of English spoken primarily by nonblacks. Of the features or Black English discussed earlier in this chapter, many of the pronunciation features of Black English occur in selected southern, regional dialects. Of the grammatical features described, all the forms except the unique use of "be" to describe intermittent events and some special forms of the verbs "do" and "have" are common in informal (nonstandard) forms of many dialects. Thus, only rarely does a linguistic item appear in the speech of one person that unmistakably labels his speech as "Black English." Actually, any particular features are as likely to indicate southern background, low social status, or a number of other factors. In sum, Black English is not a deviant language form far from other American English varieties, but a system of consistent, modulated similarities and variations within the American English family of dialects.

A final factor complicating any simplified view of Black English is that speakers of Black English may not speak Black English all the time. A speaker may use a given feature of Black English in one instance and not use it only seconds later. It would not be unusual for a child to say:

"I took it off my des' and lay it on his desk."

This is an example of simplifying a consonant cluster once and not simplifying it later in the same sentence. Almost all the features we have identified with Black English alternate in actual speech with so-called standard forms. A speaker who only uses some of the forms listed earlier about half the time is speaking 90 percent the same as an English teacher from central Indiana; yet he is likely to be labeled a speaker of Black English.

To summarize—what appears to an untrained listener as a deep-seated distinction between standard English and Black English seems, upon closer examination, to be a small set of differences in a sea of similarities between the language forms used by black and white children. The plain fact is that some black children use a relatively *small number* of uniquely Black English features in their speech *part of the time.* When these features appear they "call attention to themselves," because in the old view of language Black English features were considered deviations from the correct rules of proper speech. In the old view, using nonstandard speech features was a lot like a baseball player running to *third* base after hitting the ball. Not only would such an event be a violation of the rules, but it could be regarded as a stupid, careless error that makes winning less likely. The new view of language, by contrast, sees Black English features as alternate forms that are logical, consistent, intelligible means of communication.

SPEECH STYLES IN BLACK ENGLISH

If Black English is linguistically so similar to other dialects, why does it sound so different? The answer is that Black English and standard English often differ in how they adjust to situational influences. Nobody speaks the same way all the time. A child speaks differently to his teacher than to his brother; differently to a stranger than to a friend; and differently to the same person in a *formal* setting (church, formal dinner party, formal lecture-discussion) than in an *informal* setting (picnic, informal discussion, volley-ball game at recess). Speakers customarily take such variation for granted, yet we easily can overlook its influence on Black English usage. For example, if a lower-class, black child is interviewed in a rather formal setting, he may appear quite reticent and nonverbal. The following interview of nine-year-old Charles illustrates how the social setting can affect speech patterns.

> Charles, what I want uh you to do is to tell me about some of the things that, uh, you do. Ah, for example, what game do you play most around school? You want to tell me about that?
>
> *Charles:* Basketball.
>
> All right, and any others that you play?
>
> No, sir.
>
> Uh hum, you play any other games around your . . . uh . . . home?
>
> Kickball.
>
> What kind of ball?
>
> Kickball.
>
> Kickball, um huh. Uh now uh, tell me about this kickball, what, what's that?
>
> Uh, in kickball, well, you run to bases, straight bases, go out there, just to touch you with the ball, an' then you're out. In one way.
>
> In one way? Now you say you kick the ball did you say?
>
> Yes.
>
> I see, you like that sort of game? How do the kids play that? Uh do they seem to like it?
>
> Yes.

Um hum. Do you uh uh, now you play basketball also, uh, around your back yard.

Sometimes. I got it in my back yard.

In your back yard, uh hum. You want to tell me something about your back yard? You got a basketball uh court or something in your back yard?

No sir, I think I have a basketball goal.

A goal, I see, uh, do the kids come over and play with you?

Yes, sir.

Can you tell me anything else about kickball, basketball? The kids, are they pretty good kids? What kind of kids are they? Kids that you play with.

They're nice, and I like to play with them.

What is it you like most about playing with them, Charles?

Well, they don't try to start up no fights.

It would be a mistake to believe that Black English is merely the colloquial speech of black Americans. Rather, it is a range of stylistic usages from formal to informal, sometimes used by many Black Americans, and often displaying the features listed earlier in this chapter. In that strict sense, standard English is less a dialect than a prestigious, formal *style of usage.*

Style of usage refers to ways that speakers adjust what they say to make it most appropriate to the setting. Like Charles's speech, any child's speech varies according to the social situation. He switches styles for each occasion and therefore speaks in a number of different ways. In formal settings he may act timid. In peer-group play his speech may be enthusiastic and colloquial. At dinner, his speech may be careful, yet expressive.

Some characteristics that appear in the so-called nonstandard speech of many black children and of many lower-class white children are stylistic features, not features of a dialect. Perhaps the most important feature of colloquial style is that speaker and listener share background information and assumptions that are part of the meanings being communicated. If two children are talking informally about a television program, for example, they very likely will name isolated events in a fashion that is somewhat cryptic to an outsider. They may not mention the name of the program; they may not discuss the point of the plot; they may not even mention that they are discussing television. These items are part of the context already known by both children, so that what they say to each other within this context is quite clear to them. Yet their conversation may be unintelligible to someone who is not aware of that context.

Commonly, informal speech is used between friends, relatives, lovers— any people who know each other well enough to share background information for topics of conversation. Under such circumstances every detail need not be specified to get a message across. Further, among good friends and relatives, a speaker may feel sufficiently comfortable and secure that he need not be quite so careful or precise in his speech. Under such circumstances, speakers are likely to switch from careful, formal "school talk" modes of expression to less prestigious, nonstandard modes and colloquial "in-group" expressions. All speakers—white and black, rich and poor—shift styles from formal to informal in such circumstances, and their speech at such time shows:

1. Less specification of details of contextual background.
2. More use of nonstandard speech forms.

Examples of such style shifting can be seen in any schoolroom. During such language exercises as reading, children enunciate more clearly and use fewer nonstandard forms than they do while playing ball. Similarly, children playing games of which all know the rules may specify few details of context.

Some teachers have argued that black children need help in learning to "style shift." This is generally untrue, although some black children from lower socioeconomic class backgrounds tend not to shift styles as easily or effectively as middle-class children do under some circumstances. One researcher found that when lower-class children talked with interviewers about television programs they mentioned only isolated events, rather than outlining "what the show was about." Listeners who had not seen the shows had difficulty understanding the lower-class children's discussions due to the lack of shared background context. Middle-class children, on the other hand, often used descriptions to fill in the context.

In summary, a major difference between informal speech and formal speech is how much the speaker and listener share contextual background information. When there is low shared context speech is formal, elaborated, and detailed; and there is a tendency toward prestige linguistic forms (standard English). When there is high shared context between speaker and listener speech is informal, colloquial, and difficult for outsiders to understand; and it exhibits nonstandard language forms. All children reveal evidence of such style shifting in their speech, but middle-class children show more pronounced elaboration in formal settings than do lower-class children. This may be due to more varied experience as a function of having more money and leisure time.

What does this mean in the classroom? When a child speaks to the teacher in class, it is a formal situation. Standard, elaborated speech is usually the most appropriate style. This gives the middle-class child some advantage. Since black people in America tend to be poor, many black children are sometimes at a disadvantage in this respect. But this disadvantage is in no way a function of Black English. Rather, it is a result of the fact that the formal speech of lower-class children is less different from their informal speech than is the formal speech of middle-class children.

Finally, it should be noted that extended elaboration on the part of middle-class children is a slightly mixed blessing. Simply put, middle-class children sometimes talk too much! They may supply elaborated speech whether it is appropriate or not, making them superverbally boring. Researchers have found, for example, that lower-class children *do* supply elaborated answers to questions that clearly ask for them (e.g., "How do you play basketball?") but supply brief, more simple answers to simpler questions (e.g., "Do you play baseball?"). Middle-class children, on the other hand, are more likely to supply elaborated answers to *both* kinds of questions. They talk a lot, whether it is appropriate or not. In such a case, the lower-class child's speech is better adapted to the situation.

With the concept of style shifting in mind, note below three samples of Black speech that probably are more typical than those of Eldridge or Charles. These samples show a small number of uniquely Black-English features, but these rarely affect intelligibility.

Do you have a bicycle? Do you ride your bicycle very much?

Tyrone (age 10): I don't have no bicycle.

You don't have one?

I have a trail bike.

Trail bike, is that like a motorcycle?

Uh-huh, it's like one, but it's more littler.

It has an engine on it, though?

Uh huh.

Boy, I bet that's fun. Where do you go on it?

Up there by um . . . up there . . . what's that . . . Springdale Garden. I go in back of Springdale Garden and ride up that trail.

Uh-hun . . . Have you ever had any wrecks on it?

Uh hum, one time.

Tell me about that.

I hit a rock, and then I flew off and I cut myself. I had to get stitches in my arm.

Ooo, gosh! I bet that really hurt. Did you have to go to the hospital?

Uh huh. I had to get stiches; the glass was real sharp and it cut . . . cut my . . . cut myself real deep.

Do you have a scar on your arm from that?

Uh huh. Right there.

Ooo, What did you think about the hospital?

Uh . . . it was all right.

Were you scared when you were at the hospital?

Yeh.

What were you thinking when you were there?

I was thinking about . . . I didn't know if they're gonna put me to sleep but . . . I was thinking about I was gonna be awoke when they was . . . um sewing me up.

Oh, did that you make you scared?

Yeah, I told my mother I didn't want to get stitches. And she told me I had to if I wanted to let it keep on bleeding cause I had a bandage on.

Uh huh, so did they put you to sleep?

Uh huh.

And then did you wake up and it was all sewn up?

Yeh.

Did you spend the night in the hospital?

Uh huh. Then about a week . . . I think about two months they took it off.

Took your stitches out?

Uh-huh. Then it was well.

Bet you were glad then. Do you still ride your minibike up there?

Huh? Uh-um, I have to fix the motor.

Tyrone's family lives in a modest, middle-class neighborhood. Some observers may feel that if a child's family has enough money to buy a mini-bike, his speech could hardly be typical of most black children. So, to make the point more forcefully, listen again to Eldridge and Charles who live in a low-income, inter-city neighborhood.

Some teachers who have listened to tapes of Tyrone and other black children are rather surprised at how easily understood their speech is. Our final example is of ten-year-old Kevin, who lives in a rural, southern

town. Notice how Kevin combines features of southern regional dialect (e.g., "Ben" is pronounced "Bin") with some features of Black English. It is important to remember that black children can be expected to exhibit regional and social dialect features as well as potentially ethnic ones.

Okay, what kind of games uh, do you play around your house?

Kevin (age 10): Basketball and baseball.

Okay, which one do you enjoy playing the most?

Baseball.

Why is it you enjoy playing baseball the most?

Cause, I like to hit the ball over the fence a lot.

Do you enjoy the running part of baseball?

Yes.

Um . . . do you win a lot?

Mostly, and most usually not.

Oh, do you have a good team, or are you a good player?

I'm a good player.

Oh, well that's nice to know. Kevin, do you have any pets?

Yeah, a German, a German Shepard.

You do, well what's your dog's name?

Ben.

Ben, how old is Ben?

A year old.

Is he a mean dog or a bad dog?

Both.

Both? Well why don't you tell me about some of the things Ben has done?

Well, when we put the clothes on the line, he grabs my pants and pulls 'em down.

Just your pants?

My brother's, too!

INTELLIGIBILITY:
WHY CAN'T I UNDERSTAND BLACK SPEECH?

Some people, including teachers, state flatly that they are unable to understand the speech of black children. If there really is a serious loss of information between child speakers of Black English and their teachers, such a loss could be a barrier to effective instruction. Yet the discussion of Black English in this chapter suggests that linguistic variation between Black English and other dialects should not present severe intelligibility problems. What, then, causes claims that speakers and nonspeakers of Black English are not intelligible to each other? We suggest that there are at least five reasons for this problem, and each deserves mention.

1. *Jive talk.*   Nonstandard forms of Black English are most apparent in the speech of teen-age males. It must be noted that teen-age males of all racial backgrounds often tend to exhibit rebellious, unpredictable behavior and to become embroiled in disciplinary conflicts with teachers. Teen-age males often concoct "hip-talk," secret modes of expression for the purpose of peer-group interaction (often concerning taboo topics) that cannot be understood by parents and teachers.

The point is that any teen-age boy can make his speech unintelligible to adult outsiders. The fact that a teacher observes black children and teenagers talking jive talk that adults cannot understand should not be taken as evidence that Black English is a foreign language. As long as teachers and their students can make meanings clear to each other *when they wish to do so,* differences in language code between Black English and other dialects should not cause serious communication problems.

2. *Differences in nonverbal code.*   Sometimes nonlinguistic uses of the body convey meanings that differ according to cultural contexts. For example, when a teacher verbally rebukes a child for some transgression, some children look straight at the teacher to show subservience to authority and attention to the scolding. A child who looks away from the teacher would be demonstrating inattentiveness. Some American black children, on the other hand, often avert the eyes from the speaker as a sign of deference. To look the speaker in the eye would be to appear rebellious. A teacher unaware of this cultural difference in nonverbal expression might be insulted if a black child averted his or her gaze during a scolding. An authoritarian teacher might demand that the child look at him or her, which would indicate to the child that the teacher was encouraging rebelliousness.

Anthropologist Roger Abrahams points out another subcultural communication difference between blacks and whites in America. In black cultural groups, members of an audience listening to a public speech demonstrate interest in the message by verbal participation in the event (e.g., the stereotype of the congregation's participation in an all-black church). A teacher hearing verbal feedback during a lesson might classify it as unruly behavior, demonstrating the child's lack of interest. A black child, however, might think that to be silent is to show boredom. Thus, a teacher's commands to be quiet could be interpreted as orders not to be interested.

3. *Language loyalty.*   The old view of standard English holds that it is the only "proper" dialect, encompassing all correct and elegant ways of speaking. This attitude probably remains a serious barrier to mutual understanding between white teachers and black children. Most people teaching today (including the authors) were taught early that standard English was the only correct, careful mode of speech and that other ways of speaking were careless, sloppy, and imprecise. We were taught a strong *language loyalty* to standard English, and adherence to the school's role in teaching it. Language loyalty is a term coined by anthropoloigst John Gumperz, who has studied social uses of language in many cultures around the world. Gumperz reports that loyalty to one dialect of a language commonly causes speakers of that dialect to claim that they cannot understand other dialects that are "grammatically almost identical" to theirs. Gumperz concludes that the resulting lack of understanding is a social problem—a problem of attitudes—not a language problem.

Let us attempt to describe the effects of language loyalty in more concrete terms. A child in a fifth-grade history class responds to a direct question with the following utterance.

"Columbus, he discover America in 1492."

The teacher feels a slight visceral tension, language loyalty is aroused. The teacher is fairly sure that he or she should correct the child's "grammar" to prevent such a "mistake" from recurring. So the teacher repeats the child's sentence, emphasizing the portions corrected. What has happened?

First, the teacher has switched the lesson from history to English. The history lesson suffers, not because disciplines should be kept separate in school but because the *correct historical content* of the child's response has gone unrecognized.

Second, the child's grammar is unlikely to "improve" as a result of this teaching strategy.

Third, no matter how kindly the teacher phrases the correction, he has belittled the child by responding to the superficial form of the utterance (over which the child has little conscious control) rather than to its content (which demonstrates that the child has been attending to the lesson). Suppose the child had responded:

"Columbus discovered America in 1492."

If in the tension of the moment, the child had slumped nervously in his chair and scratched his elbow, what would you think of the teacher who replied, "Henry, please stop scratching and slouching when you answer"? We probably would find it regrettable that the teacher focused on irrelevant surface behaviors instead of on rewarding a correct response. This situation

is similar to correcting Black English in the classroom, except that because of our training and socialization in language loyalty, most teachers find it difficult to see that such forms are in many cases superficial behaviors. How much better it is to have the child say, "Columbus, he discover America in 1492," than, "I believe it is correct to assume that Marco Polo discovered Brooklyn in 1848."

Finally, and most importantly, the teacher in this example may actually have failed to understand the child's Black English utterance because he reacted primarily to the "mistakes" in it. Thus, the teacher who listened to the error rather than the sentence's meaning literally did not understand the Black English. Yet the fault for this misunderstanding lies as much in the teacher's language loyalty as in the child's sentence. Suppose a child says, "Atomic bombs, they be cool," and his teacher responds only by correcting his grammar. We would argue that both teacher and student have failed to derive maximum benefit from the situation.

4. *Speaking Black English.* Because of their backgrounds, few white teachers can speak Black English without special effort. This may lead to a feeling by students as well as teachers that differences between Black English and standard English are very large. But when one stops to think about it, the way a person speaks is tied in complex ways to his or her individual personality, to his values, and to his cultural background. Everyone sounds uniquely like himself or herself. It would be as difficult for a white teacher to sound like John Wayne or Archie Bunker as to speak Black English. Sounding black or sounding like John Wayne would be a put-on, artificial, an imitation.

This does not mean there is an important language problem between white teachers and black students, any more than there is between the same teacher and John Wayne. The important point is that despite dialect differences white teachers and black students are able to *comprehend* messages sent by each other. Clearly, speakers of Black English can understand messages in other dialects and vice versa.

Therefore, it would be a mistake for white teachers to attempt to address their black students in Black English. Rather, they should appreciate the speech diversity of various students, since it reflects culture and personality. The teacher should speak in a manner naturally reflective of his or her culture and personality, expecting the same kind of appreciation for that speech as he or she demonstrates for the speech of others. Children may come to admire and copy such a teacher, which may be the only realistic method for "teaching" standard English.

5. *Bigotry.* We hate to admit it, but some teachers are bigots. The nonstandard forms spoken by black students appear distinctive to bigoted teachers largely because of the speaker's race. One of the most obvious characteristics of a genuinely bigoted teacher is that he or she probably would not read this book.

SOME PRACTICAL SUGGESTIONS

We have simplified some linguistic issues in this chapter and have
shown that problems of communication between black children and
their white teachers are not fundamentally "language problems." Many
linguists agree that the problems are not linguistic. Rather, people use
language attitudes as a handle for describing social problems. We do not
mean to imply that these social problems are trivial. They just aren't
language problems. We also have simplified our examples of interactions
between children and teachers and challenged teachers to learn new
perspectives. We do not mean to imply that present teachers are doing a
bad job. On the contrary, we find teachers to be resourceful, energetic,
underpaid, and idealistic. Our point is that teachers must understand the
following: Black English is a dialect like any other—*not* a mental handicap.
Standard English is a style that any speaker of any dialect is likely to use.

How do we teach language?   This question is a tough one. Perhaps
there is no way to "teach" language consciously. It is fortunate that normal
children learn language, no matter what teachers do. The best instruction in
language seems to be to engage the student in fascinating, meaningful
conversation for "talk practice." Sometimes, linguistic games—rhyming,
punning, and so on—are helpful. Certainly, correcting the child's speech or
grammar does not teach language and it has undesirable side effects as
well.

When does a child know standard English style?   If we agree that
children should learn standard English style, how can we teach that; and
how can we tell whether a given child "knows" it? We do not have good
evidence about how to teach styles of speech, though it seems that
manipulating situational variables through games, dramatic play, and field
trips are helpful exercises. Teachers or parents can tell that a child "knows"
a language code or style when he gives clear indication that he *understands*
it. Then, when he sometimes uses a particular form in his speech, he
"knows" it still better. Do not be discouraged that some forms of undesired
speech are slow to disappear entirely. The problem of learning new speech
styles rarely is one of not knowing how to use the proper form; it simply is
one of not actually employing it on some occasions, perhaps for a variety
of reasons.

Does a child need to know standard English style in order to read? It
probably helps. But by now you should recognize that this is a very different
question than whether a child needs to know standard English *dialect.*
Nearly all writing is in standard English style; and the more facile a child is
with that style, the better he or she is likely to read. All Black English

speakers *know* standard English style to some degree. The problem is not to teach a "new style of speech" to someone ignorant of it, but to foster greater range and eloquence in a style that is already "known" and understood.

The practice of teaching reading by reading aloud sometimes causes problems for child speakers of Black English. A child might see the following sentence:

"Jim is going home."

and say it so that it sounds like:

"Jim going home."

A teacher unfamiliar with Black English might think that the child missed or misread the word "is." It is more likely that the child pronounced the sentence in Black English, slurring the words "Jim" and "is" together (as is common in any dialect) then deleting the "s" as the final consonant in a cluster. More important than the detailed dialect background of the child's pronunciation is the obvious fact that the child read and understood the sentence. If the teacher corrects the speech rendering of that sentence the teacher is in the position of correcting trivial, surface behavior while failing to reward correct content. The entire practice of correcting "mistakes" in reading aloud may be of questionable value to speakers of any dialect. Reading, after all, is primarily for understanding, not for diction practice.

What about the times when I still can't understand?   When teachers and students possess different cultural backgrounds and speak different dialects, some misunderstandings are human and inevitable. When such problems occur, we suggest the following four-step procedure for tracking down causes.

1. Try to specify as much context as possible—of all parties concerned.
2. Closely examine the teacher's attitudes toward the child, the child's race, and most of all—toward standard English.
3. Examine potential cultural differences between teacher and child that could lead to misinterpretation.
4. If the teacher rarely has heard Black English spoken before, there may be some dialect interference. Practice in communicating with Black children should take care of this problem.

SUGGESTED ACTIVITIES

1. Listen again to the segment in which Eldridge discusses being saved. Do not look at the transcript. Make a mark on a piece of paper every time he says something you cannot understand. What does the number of marks you made indicate? Are you able to understand Eldridge's basic meanings? What does that suggest to you?

2. Of the children you heard in this chapter, who seems most typical of the black children to whom you have listened and talked? How do you explain this in terms of: a. yourself, b. the situation, and c. the child? When considering your own role, consider the categories of possible misunderstanding that are discussed at the close of this chapter.

3. Play the segment of Charles's speech again. Play it when you are alone. Close your eyes and pretend you are Charles. What are you feeling? What do you think about the man who is interviewing you? What do you figure is probably the purpose of the interview?

4. Develop a list of at least a dozen words used in Black English that most non-speakers of this dialect would not understand. Do they center around any certain types of subject matter?

5. If you are a speaker of Black English or work with some, develop a role-playing situation where style shifting between standard and Black English is required. What types of roles and situations seem most relevant.

6. Set up a simulated meeting of parents who represent both speakers and non-speakers of Black English along with school officials where the topic is how, or if, Black English is to be used in the classroom. What key arguments emerge?

The Native, Spanish-Speaking Child

5

I remember the time I went to see a doctor. I had problem with my big toe. The receptionist asked me where I lived, my name, and what was wrong with me. I had . . . I told her that I . . . my foot . . . my fat thumb was hurting. She look at my right thumb and said, "I don't see anything wrong with it." "Oh, yes, it hurting, my big thumb, not that one but the other." She repeated the operation and said, "It looks all right to me." "Miss, it's not this thumb or that thumb, but my *big* thumb." "Well, I still don't see anything wrong with it," she said. "Miss, this is my big thumb," and I removed my shoe, and show her my right foot toe.

THE PROBLEM

Carlos, who was talking about himself, is one of more than 10 million persons of Spanish-speaking backgrounds in the United States—including an estimated 1.5 million Puerto Ricans, concentrated in the New York and New England area; some one-half million Cubans, living mainly in Florida; and more than 5 million Mexican-Americans, concentrated in the southwestern states.

When Carlos started school more than 15 years ago he spoke almost no English, and his parents' English was limited to such expressions as, "Thank you" and "Good morning." In spite of an inability to speak and understand English, Carlos and children like him were expected to perform in an English-speaking, first-grade classroom, sometimes in segregated schools or classrooms and sometimes in competition with children who spoke English as natives. Speaking Spanish was forbidden, and Carlos and his Spanish-speaking friends knew that they would be disciplined if discovered using Spanish on the school grounds. Carlos and his friends were given books in English and were expected to learn to read from them, even though their words meant nothing to them. The world of Dick, Jane, Spot, and Puff was not their world, and they were not provided the prerequisite linguistic and conceptual background to enter that world. They remained outsiders during much of their elementary schooling, and in many ways it was made clear to them that teachers would put up with them only on the school's terms. It wasn't that educators intended to mistreat Mexican-American children; they believed that it was in the best interest of the school, the American educational system, and the Spanish-speaking child to place him in a totally English-speaking environment so that he would be integrated into the "dominant" culture as quickly as possible.

As might be expected, prohibiting the use of Spanish and insisting on the use of English more often hindered than aided the learning process. In most cases, Spanish-speaking children suffered in other ways, too. They sometimes were considered "nonverbal," unable to speak any language. For this reason, they were seated off to one side of the room, where they would not be expected to participate in classroom activities, where gradually they could be forgotten. Or, they were sent to special classes, because their inability to speak English was interpreted as a sign of retardation. Although it may seem incredible to us today, children who were forbidden to speak the language they *knew* were judged to be retarded because they did not speak a language they *did not know*. Although times have changed and educators have made great strides in improving the general educational environment for the Spanish-speaking child, we still occasionally hear of a child who—because of a non-English-speaking background—is diagnosed and placed in a special education classroom. We hear of school districts that formerly prohibited Spanish and still actively discourage its use anywhere on the school grounds. Fortunately, these cases quickly are becoming the exception.

The results of educational practices at the time Carlos entered school were quite predictable. Carlos and most of his friends came to dislike school, to put in their time because they were obliged to by their parents or by law. They dropped out of school as soon as possible. The drop-out rate of Mexican-American students is much higher than that of their "Anglo"[1] counterparts in the same geographical area. Although 85 percent of all Anglo children in the southwestern states complete the 12th grade,

[1] In most southwestern states with large Mexican-American populations white, English-speaking children are referred to as "Anglos."

only 60 percent of Mexican-American children do. And nearly 24 percent of Anglos, but only 5.4 percent of Mexican-Americans complete college. Although we focus here on Mexican-Americans, they can be considered characteristic of Spanish-speaking populations in general. That is, the dropout rate of children of Spanish-speaking backgrounds—be they Mexican-American, Puerto Rican, or Cuban—is considerably higher than that of native English-speaking children.

Let us consider now Susan who is eight years old and in the second grade. Like Carlos, Susan spoke little or no English before coming to school. At home, Susan's family continues to speak only Spanish.

Susan, is it good to know how to speak English and Spanish?

Susan: Yes, cause some of the peoples talk English and we don't understand them.

What does your mother do?

She stay at home and clean the house.

Where is she right now?

On the house.

What do your brothers . . . where are your brothers and sisters now?

At Zavala School.

What are they doing?

Learning.

Okay, Susan, what do you do at home to help your mother?

Clean . . . uh . . . clean the house.

And what do your brothers and sisters do to help your mother?

Clean the babies.

BILINGUAL EDUCATION

Although the linguistic attitudes and practices in Susan's home environment now are not much different from those in Carlos's home when he began first grade more than 15 years ago, school attitudes and practices certainly have changed. In the years that elapsed between Carlos's and Susan's entrance to first grade, educational planners gradually began to recognize the importance of developing programs especially designed for native Spanish-speaking children. This includes special classes in English as a second language as well as bilingual programs to foster the study of the native language and culture as well as the language and traditions of the the English-speaking world. In the state of Texas, for example, bilingual education began in 1969 with 19 projects serving 10,000 children. It grew to 40 projects serving 43,000 children by 1973. Nationally, such bilingual educational television series for children as *Carrascolendas* and *Villa Alegre* have been developed and broadcast. Thus, in a relatively short period of time, serious attempts have been made to revise and redefine the education of Spanish-speaking children. In this redefinition, Spanish is no longer prohibited; instead it is considered a valuable asset that should be acknowledged and enhanced in the educational setting.

The rapidly occurring changes in educational policies concerning the Spanish-speaking child have not themselves been without problems. One of the problems has been determining which children will benefit most from particular instructional programs. For example, some programs concentrate on a systematic presentation of English as a second language and the initial presentation of content material (e.g., mathematics) in Spanish until the child's competence in English permits him to study it in English. Candidates for such a program sometimes were (and in some cases *are* even now) selected on the sole basis of surname. That is, a child named Gomez was an automatic candidate for such a bilingual program. But surname is hardly a reliable indicator of language competence. If you take a moment to consider the ethnic background of people you know as revealed in their surnames, you know that you do not expect a friend named Schneider to speak German, nor one named LaRue to speak French. Why, then, should someone named Gomez be expected to speak Spanish? Well, he shouldn't; and in many cases, he doesn't. Let us now consider Mary Beth, who has a Spanish surname and is from the same region as Carlos and Susan. Mary Beth's parents both speak English; and they make every effort to use that language with their children, because they feel strongly that not knowing English will be a great educational and occupational handicap.

Like what rules do you use for a fair fight?

Not to fight.

But you're already fighting, aren't you?

I know, I mean for big people. And big people.

What do you mean by big people? Just big people, huh?

Well, they can get in jail.

Big people get in jail?

Yes.

How do they get in jail?

Well, sometimes they get in a fight, and sometimes they get a ticket.

If you saw someone kicking somebody else who had fallen down, what would you do?

I'd call the policemans.

You'd call the policeman?

Yes.

But meanwhile the policeman is coming over here, what would you do?

Huh?

Meanwhile, the time the policeman's taking, you know, to get over here, what would you do?

Um ... . I'd call other policeman.

Wouldn't you do anything?

Yes.

On your own?

Yes.

Like what?

Uh, tell them to not fight.

Would you go help him?

Yes.

In what way would you help him?

God's way.

In what way?

God's.

In God's way?

Yes.

Like, what do you mean in God's way?

Well, I'd help him in God's way, and sometimes I help him in my way.

The error of placing Mary Beth in a program where content material is taught in Spanish should be obvious. Since she is for all practical purposes a monolingual English speaker, her education would be disrupted by the decision that she would learn best in Spanish because of her surname.

Susan and Mary Beth are examples of extreme points on a scale that ranges from children who, like Susan, are monolingual Spanish speakers upon entering school to those like Mary Beth who are monolingual English speakers. Between these two endpoints, there are seemingly endless variations. That is, there are children who are dominant in Spanish but who know a considerable amount of English; children who use English most of the time and Spanish with Grandma and Grandpa; children who use English with their friends in the neighborhood and Spanish at home with their family, and so on. Some parents insist that Spanish be spoken at home so as to protect the Spanish-speaking heritage of the family from the pervasive English influence. Other parents, attempt to purse themselves and their children of any vestige of Spanish because they believe that Spanish is a handicap. In still other families, the relationship between the two languages is more informal, and switching from one to the other occurs without any conscious attention being paid to the fact.

The important result of this wide variation in the use of Spanish and English among Spanish-surnamed families in the United States is that their children cannot be considered a linguistically homogeneous group in the school setting. Each child's competence in Spanish or English is the result of all the factors (e.g., family and neighborhood practices, beliefs, attitudes, taboos) that surround him during the early years of life. In any given group of 30 children there may well be 30 different Spanish-English language competency combinations represented. As a Spanish surname does not reliably indicate language competence, nor does the fact that a child speaks some Spanish mean that he is dominant in Spanish, or that he will learn best if taught in Spanish. The placement of students in programs designed to benefit them must be carried out carefully, or the benefits will be lost and the effects counter-productive. The key to proper placement is effective language assessment—that is, testing that permits the determination of the language capabilities of each individual child, bilingual or monolingual. Essential to effective assessment and subsequent instruction is a familiarity with the linguistic systems underlying both Spanish and English.

SPANISH-ENGLISH DIFFERENCES

Before we proceed to discuss specific aspects of the Spanish and English linguistic systems, it is important to recall that like all other languages, Spanish exhibits both regional and social dialect variations. For example, the dialect of Spanish spoken by Mexican-Americans in the southwest typically differs from that spoken by Puerto Ricans in New York and from that spoken by Cubans in Miami. As you listen to this selection on the record, note the two different regional dialects of Spanish. The first is Puerto Rican and the second Mexican. We asked the speakers to read from the same passage so that the differences between their dialects would be emphasized. Even if you do not speak Spanish, you probably will detect at least some of the differences in how the two speakers pronounce specific words, much as you would detect the differences between the New England and southern American English dialects that were discussed in Chapter 3. The selection read aloud, first by a Puerto Rican and then by a Mexican, follows.

Van así una distancia y entonces se encuentran con unos hombres. Estos hombres critican al muchacho por permitir a su padre viejo y cansado ir a pie mientras él monta la burra. El padre y el hijo discuten la situatión. Les parece que los hombres tienen razón. El padre monta la burra y el hijo va a pie.

You should be able to hear the differences in pronunciation by these two Spanish speakers, such as the way they pronounce the *s* at the end of syllables (*esta, bestia, unos, hombres*) and the *rr* sound in *burra*. There are also differences in grammar and vocabulary that reading the same material does not permit us to demonstrate. The point is, however, that the dialects do differ.

In spite of the differences that occur in the dialects of Cubans, Mexicans, and Mexican-Americans or in those of Mexican-Americans in Texas and those in California, all of these people are speaking Spanish. The sound system, the grammar, and the vocabulary are clearly Spanish. Some people criticize the Spanish spoken by Mexican-Americans or by Puerto Ricans, because—they claim—it is not real Spanish but an amalgam of English and Spanish, a linguistic aberration called "Spanglish." Listen to Luis, who tells us a story in what might be considered such an amalgam. As you listen, try to determine what it is about Luis's speech that leads to criticism by some people. You can tell some of this from reading the selection, even if you do not know much Spanish. Is he speaking all Spanish?

Un día fue, a, Rudolfo pasando por la calle, y nomás fue andando, y de ahí de repente miró a un senor que da tarjetitas. Y de repente el senor le dio una y él ni supo. Y de ahí, pues, fue andando, y de ahí, a, miró que la car . . . tarjeta, a, dijía, "la puerta verde." Pues se fue para allá, y fue para el office y en la . . . pues . . . en la first floor ahí estaba y miró que se iba para dentist, y de ahí . . . so . . . subió para la second floor. Y de ahí miró estaban, a, pues era una tienda donde venden, a sombreros, you know, . . . asina . . . y de ahí se fue para la . . . para la otra floor de . . . y miró la puerta verde y de ahí naquió.

Even if you do not know Spanish, you undoubtedly noticed that Luis used such English words as *office, dentist, first floor,* and *you know.* Another interesting feature of this sample is the use of the past tense verb *naquió,* derived from the English verb *knock.* But although Luis's speech contains borrowings from English, there is no doubt that he is speaking Spanish. Spanish speakers generally will understand him, and English speakers will not. The sentence structure (syntax) and the form of almost all words (including naquió) is Spanish.

People who hold the view that speakers like Luis are not speaking Spanish are either ignorant of how language works or are using language to criticize people against whom they are prejudiced on other grounds. Indeed, as we discussed in Chapter 3, two languages that coexist in a given area are bound to affect each other. Thus, Spanish speakers in the southwestern United States might talk of the "brecas" used to stop their cars, and English speakers in the same area might speak of having "chilly con carny" for dinner. No one would accuse the English speaker of speaking "Spanglish" because he happens to talk about the spicy food he enjoys. But the Spanish speaker often is not given the same benefit of the doubt when he talks about the brakes on his car. As discussed in Chapter 3, each dialect of a language has a context in which it is most appropriate, and teachers who work with native, Spanish-speaking children must be willing to acknowledge the dialect of Spanish these children speak.

Another implication of the dialect variation within the Spanish-speaking world is that these variations must be considered when planning a program and choosing materials. The change from monolingual to bilingual educational programs meant that materials in Spanish were required suddenly, and they were not readily available. One solution was to seek out materials from Spanish-speaking countries. Another was to develop custom-made materials that—because of the demand for such materials— were then shared with programs for which they were not custom made. There are both linguistic and cultural differences that may make materials designed for one Spanish-speaking population inappropriate for another. (Consider the problems that might arise if we attempted to incorporate books published in England in our elementary school curriculum.) Although educators have been quick to criticize the "Dick and Jane solution" to the educational problem of the Spanish-speaking in the United States, they have viewed far less critically inappropriate Argentine or Venezuelan solutions to the same problem.

The challenge that the Spanish-speaking (*not* necessarily the Spanish-surnamed) child presents is one requiring a sound knowledge of how Spanish operates and how it is similar to and different from English. To place children in appropriate educational settings, to provide them with educational activities and materials that will maximize their learning of both languages and of content areas, those working with the children must know something about how both languages work. You must be able to design assessment instruments to determine the child's level of competence in each of the two languages, the dominance of one language over another, and the effects of the interference of one language on the other. You also must be able to develop instructional materials and procedures that will facilitate the Spanish-speaking child's acquisition of English. Teachers or parents of Spanish-speaking children should be able to determine whether materials and procedures that are developed or suggested by others are appropriate to the child's locale; if they are inappropriate they must be able to adapt them to fit the setting. To have a chance at doing all these things well, you must have a knowledge of how English and Spanish work, of how they are similar, how they are different, and of how knowledge of one may enhance or interfere with the acquisition of the other. The rest of this chapter will discuss briefly

Spanish and English sounds, spelling, grammatical patterns, and vocabulary. We will present an overview of some of the language features that may occur in the English of children who speak Spanish as natives. Since not all Spanish speakers who learn English are alike, not all of the points in the ensuing pages will necessarily be characteristic of all the Spanish-speaking children with whom you come in contact. In fact, it would be highly unlikely that you would find all these features in the speech of one given individual. Nevertheless, with this general overview you should be able to identify some of the specific features of a child's English that may result from a Spanish-speaking background and to understand some of the reasons why they occur in his or her speech.

SOUNDS

In the area of sound articulation, there are two extreme points of view that should be considered at the outset. In the first place, there sometimes is a tendency to overemphasize the teaching of the exact articulation of given sounds in a specific language. Children are forced to spend hours repeating words and drilling sounds until they approach some state of articulatory perfection. We sometimes find six-year-olds without their front teeth being drilled in the production of the *th* sound (as in teeth), when front teeth are essential to successfully produce this sound. At the opposite extreme are those who argue that teaching the articulation of English sounds to Spanish speakers is not important at all, because speaking English with a Spanish accent usually does not result in misunderstanding.

Although it is true that in most cases accented speech does not cause a complete breakdown in communication and that people like Maurice Chevalier and Henry Kissinger have done very well with their accents, misunderstandings do occur from time to time. For example, a native Spanish-speaking university student once told us that her cat was "deceased." After expressing our sympathies, we discovered that the cat was ill (diseased), not dead. In this case, the difference between life and death depended upon her successful articulation of the *z* sound. Another native Spanish-speaking student surprised his teacher by informing her that he had a lot of trouble with his "bowels." Before she could react to this information, he specified that the "bowels" that gave him the most trouble were the "a" in *cat* and the "u" in *cut*. We are happy to report that the teacher quickly recovered her composure. These are but two of many examples of possible misunderstandings that occur because of the substitution of sounds. Often, the context in which the "accented" word occurs resolves the possible ambiguity or confusion; but—as in the two cases just mentioned—the context is not always adequate. Another, and possibly more important, reason that sounds are important is that people judge other people by the way they speak (see Chapter 6). Although Henry Kissinger's accent may be considered attractive, a job seeker's may not. We are not suggesting that everyone articulate all sounds the same way. We already have seen in Chapter 3 that although native English speakers often sound very different from each other, confusion seldom results. And we certainly should not expect of native Spanish-speaking children what we never expect of their English-speaking classmates, i.e., that they learn to articulate English sounds in some exact way. On the other hand, there are certain sounds in the English of native Spanish speakers that are very difficult for us to ignore. They confuse us, and sometimes we even become irritated because we must work to understand them. Spanish-speaking children who are learning English should not be drilled to sound exactly like Walter Cronkite or even like their English teacher; but an effort should be made to teach them English sounds so they are not misjudged by those with whom they will come in contact later in their lives, and so they do not feel uncomfortable about speaking English whenever they want or need to do so.

Problem sounds.   There are certain English sounds (e.g., the *th* in *with*) that frequently present problems to six-year-old, English-speaking children. Children's usual strategy for dealing with these difficult sounds is to substitute other sounds for them; instead of *with,* they may say *wif,* as in, "I want to go wif you." Because substitutions like *wif* for *with* are very common among six-year-old, native English-speaking children and because maturing children regularly are observed to acquire this sound without rigorous training in its articulation, the difficulty in articulating such sounds probably can be attributed to the speaker's immaturity.

When native Spanish-speaking children begin learning English they, too, are observed to make certain sound substitutions. Like their English-speaking classmates they are likely to say *wif* for *with* because they, too, are immature speakers. On the other hand, Spanish-speaking children seem to have difficulty with certain other English sounds, making substitutions for them that are not observed in their English-speaking classmates. For example, they may say *chew* instead of *shoe* or *cheap* for *sheep.* This substitution of *ch* for *sh* is observed regularly in the English of native Spanish-speaking children but usually not observed in the speech of native English-speaking children of the same age; thus, it cannot be attributed to immaturity. We reasonably may suggest then, that there is something about Spanish that may be influencing the Spanish speaker's pronunciation of the *sh* in *shoe* and *sheep* to make it sound more like the *ch* in *chew* or *cheap.* By isolating such examples as these, we can determine which sounds seem difficult for most young children, be they English or Spanish-speaking, and which seem to occur almost exclusively in the English of native Spanish speakers.

Another way we can distinguish between sound substitutions in English that result from the speaker's immaturity and those resulting from speaking Spanish as natives, is to listen to the sound substitutions that occur in the English of a mature, native Spanish speaker. Immaturity clearly can be ruled out as the possible origin of difficulties with certain sounds in this instance. Gilberto is a mature (16-year-old) speaker. The sound substitutions in his English probably can be attributed to his having spoken Spanish before acquiring English, and they are representative of the substitutions that will be discussed later in this chapter.

> I have a frie*nd*, a family friend in Tucson, Arizona, and they are my . . . they are my friends . . . all the family. And . . and *they* in*v*ite . . in*v*ite me to *s*pend the holidays eh . . perio . . . period on . . with them in Tucson, Arizona. When I . . . when I *was* in Tucson, Arizona, I . . I co*u*ld see *the* . . . *the* c*u*stoms of the . . of the most of the American people. I see *they* . . . *they* are very friendly, and . . and *they* have many differe*nt* ide*a*s like the Mexican people. When . . . when I was talking with them they told me *they* . . . *s*ince . . *s*ince Thanksgivi*ng* . . *s*ince . . since . . since . . since Thanksgivi*ng* day until . . until New Year it's a lot of fun be*c*ause they . . they love to . . to enjoy on . . on *th*is . . on *th*is holiday be*c*ause on . . on Thanksgiving day *they* said *they* . . *they* . . *they* . . *they* like to . . to prepare special food for *th*is occ*a*sion. And . . and *they* . . *they* prepare special dinner for Thanksgivi*ng*. Then *they* told me about Chri*s*tmas. *Then* I co*u*ld . . I co*u*ld . . I co*u*ld saw *they* . . *they* have . . uh . . they have tree wi*th* colorful and . . and *they* ha*v*e gifts. Also *they* ha*v*e a Santa Cla*u*s. I think *the* . . the most who enjoy in *th*is Chri*s*tmas is the . . the *ch*ild be*c*ause they believe in Santa Cla*u*s. This is an . . an . . an uh *h*istorical person who gives, who brings gift to the . . to the child. Also I *v*isit uh the *ch*ur*ch*es, the parks. I *v*isit the *desert* in Tucson, Arizona . . .

Consonants. The first thing to notice about Spanish and English consonant sounds is that there are many that—with only very slight differences in pronunciation—the two languages have in common. The following consonant sounds occur in both Spanish and English.

Sound	As in English word	As in Spanish word
p	pan	pan (bread)
b	boy	voy (I am going)
t	too	tú (you)
d	day	de (of)
k	cone	con (with)
g	goat	gota (drop)
ch	cheek	chico (small)
f	fin	fin (end)
s	sin	sin (without)

Sound	*As in English word*	*As in Spanish word*
h	howl	jaula (cage)
m	mom	mamá (mom)
n	no	no (no)
l	lay	ley (law)
w	wave	huevo (egg)
y	yellow	hielo (ice)

With all these consonant sounds common to both languages the native Spanish-speaking child already has a good start in learning the consonant sound distinctions of English. In effect, he already knows 15 English consonants, and the discrimination and articulation of these sounds should not present serious problems.

In addition to the aforementioned 15, there are nine consonant sound distinctions in English that do not occur in Spanish. It usually is these consonant distinctions that present problems to the native Spanish-speaking child.

Sound	*As in English word*
v	vote, leave
j	judge, George
z	zoo, rose
sh	ship, wish
zh	measure, television
th	thick, thin, with
Th	the, then, either
ng	sing, wrong, finger
r[2]	ready, carrot, star

The Spanish-speaking child who confronts these new sounds usually relates them to the Spanish sound that most closely resembles them. Thus, since

[2] Although the letter *r* exists in Spanish, the sounds that correspond to this letter are totally different from the English *r*. Consequently, the English *r* is not comparable to any Spanish consonant sound.

Spanish contains no *s-z* distinction, the native Spanish speaker usually will substitute *s* for *z* in English, saying *piece* for *peas, niece* for *knees,* and *Sue* for *zoo.* He or she also usually substitutes *b* for *v,* resulting in *boat* instead of *vote,* and—as we saw earlier—*bowel* for *vowel.* The *ng* that occurs at the end of many English words usually is replaced by *n;* so *sing* becomes *sin,* and *rang* becomes *ran.* A comparative examination of the consonant sound distinctions in Spanish (those in the first list plus the *ny* and the two Spanish *r* sounds) and those in English permits a fairly reliable determination of those consonant substitutions likely to occur in the English of native Spanish speakers.

Distribution of consonant sounds. Another important difference between English and Spanish involves the *position* in which certain sounds occur in a word. In general, the distribution of consonants in Spanish is more restricted than it is in English. As a result, the Spanish speaker learning English encounters not only the unfamiliar consonant sound discriminations mentioned above, but also the unexpected positions of certain consonant sounds. For example, the only consonants at the ends of words in Spanish are:

Sound	As in Spanish word
d	verdad (truth)
s	menos (less)
l	papel (paper)
r	por (for)
n	pan (bread)
y	rey (king)

None of the other Spanish consonant sounds that appeared in the first list occurs at the ends of words. In English, on the other hand, the only consonant sound that does *not* occur at the ends of words is *h.* What this means for the native, Spanish-speaking student is that he must learn to listen for and to pronounce sounds like *p, t,* and *k* at the ends of words, where he never has experienced them before. Consequently, before he learns to recognize those English final consonants that do not occur in final position in Spanish, the native Spanish speaker frequently omits them. Thus, *whip, with,* and *wick* may all sound alike to Spanish-speaking students who need training in listening for and producing these final consonant sounds.

Another characteristic of English consonants is that they often occur in groups called "clusters" or "blends." In Spanish, there are relatively few consonant clusters, and they usually occur only at the beginning of syllables or words. Thus, in Spanish there are such words as *tren* (train), *playa* (beach), *blanco* (white), *libro* (book), *grupo* (group), *precio* (price), *clase* (class), *crisis* (crisis), *gloria* (glory), *frito* (fried), *cuando* (when), and *quiero* (I want), which contain syllable-initial consonant clusters. The second consonant sound in each of these Spanish clusters is always *r, l, w,* or *y*. These same consonant clusters occur in English—*price, please, bridge, black, trick, drop, cross, class, grape, glass, free, quick,* and *cute.* Since the same clusters occur in both languages, native Spanish-speaking students should not encounter much difficulty with them in English, except perhaps for the articulation of the English *r* that occurs in some of the clusters. The English *r* also figures in such other consonant clusters, however, as *thr* in *three* and *through* and *shr* in *shrink* and *shrimp.* These are very difficult for Spanish speakers, because neither of the two consonants clusters is a sount that in the occurs in Spanish.

In addition to those already mentioned, there is in English a large group of consonant clusters that occurs at the beginning of words where *s* is the first consonant. These initial clusters include the following.

Initial cluster	As in English word
sp	spot
st	stop
sk	school
sl	slide
sm	smile
sn	snack
sw	swim
spl	split
spr	spring
str	string
skr	scream
skw	square

The only one of these *s*-initial consonant clusters that occurs in Spanish is the *sw* as in *suave* (soft). Instead of an initial *s*-cluster in Spanish, the vowel *e* frequently occurs at the beginning of a word, preceding the cluster and effectively dividing the two consonants into two separate syllables. For example, the Spanish equivalent of the word *special* (which contains two syllables and begins with the consonant cluster, *sp*) is *especial* (espesyal). Here, the initial *e* separates the following two consonants (*s* and *p*) into two separate syllables, *es-pe-syal*. The consequence of this difference is that native Spanish speakers transfer the Spanish pattern to English. Thus, such words as *school, spin,* and *stick* are pronounced as if they contained two syllables—the first containing *es* and the second the rest of the word (es-kuwl), (es-pin), and (es-tik).

We already indicated above that there are more consonants that may occur at the ends of words in English than there are in Spanish. Further, final consonants in English may occur singly as in *cap;* or in clusters as in *help, harp, jump, bulb, curb, heart, salt, card, child, fork, milk, warm, warn, calm, fast, grasp, ask,* and so on. No such clusters occur in Spanish. As we already have mentioned, Spanish-speaking children frequently omit single consonants in the word-final position in English because such an occurrence is not characteristic of Spanish. As might be expected, then, consonant clusters at the ends of English words present serious learning problems to the native Spanish speaker. (See the section on grammar later in this chapter for further details concerning these final consonant clusters.)

Before examining the vowel systems of English and Spanish, you might listen again to Gilberto (or to any of the other speakers you listened to earlier in this chapter), noting especially the difficulties he encounters with English consonants.

Vowel sounds.   The principal difference between English and Spanish vowels is that in English there are more vowel distinctions than there are in Spanish. The native Spanish speaker usually finds it difficult to discriminate and produce all these English vowel contrasts. Comparing the two vowel systems, the Spanish speaker's problems become clear. A comparison of the two vowel systems in the word list on page 105 will clarify some of the problems of native Spanish speakers.

The difference in the total number of vowel distinctions in the two languages means that the Spanish speaker frequently is unable to discriminate between words such as *bet, bait,* and *bat.* He also will find it difficult to pronounce *bet, bait,* and *bat* so that English speakers know which one he means. These three vowels all sound alike to him, because in Spanish a single vowel, *e,* corresponds to all three English vowel sounds.

Another important distinction between Spanish and English vowels is related to word stress and its effect on vowel quality and length. In Spanish, vowels have the same quality and length whether they are in a stressed or an unstressed syllable in a word. For example, the two vowels in *casa* (house) are the same in length and quality, although the first is in a stressed syllable and the second in an unstressed syllable. The same is true for the two vowels in *como* (as), *viví* (I lived), and *veces* (times), even though in each case one of the two vowels is stressed and the other unstressed. As a consequence of this equal vowel quality and length, Spanish often is described as having a staccato rhythm. In English, however, vowel quality and length are markedly affected by whether the vowel occurs in a stressed or unstressed syllable. A vowel occurring in an unstressed syllable often is shorter in length and in quality often resembles the vowel in the word *nut.* This change in vowel quality and length often is referred to as *vowel reduction.* For example, the word *legal* in English regularly is pronounced [li̇y:gʌl] with stress on the first syllable. The vowel in the first syllable is a long *iy*; length is indicated by the ":". In the word *legality,* on the other hand, stress is shifted to the second syllable; and the quality of the two vowels changes through the shift in stress (lʌgáe:l)-ity. The first vowel, which was a long *iy* under stress, now occurs in an unstressed syllable as a short ᴧ.[3] The second vowel, which in an unstressed syllable was a short ᴧ, now becomes a long *ae* under stress. There are many such vowel changes resulting from stress shifts in English, and English speakers automatically produce them. The Spanish speaker, accustomed as he is to a consistent vowel length and quality regardless of stress, will have difficulty in comprehending and producing words that reflect this feature of English.

English		Spanish	
Vowel sound[4]	*As in:*	*Vowel sound*	*As in:*
iy	seat	i	sin (without)
i	sit		
ey	bait	e	de (of)
e	bet		
ae	bat		
a	not	a	casa (house)
ᴧ	nut		
ɔ	caught	o	como (as)
ow	coat		
u	full	u	luna (moon)
uw	fool		

There are, of course, additional vowel problems encountered by native Spanish speakers learning English. But this brief overview should give you a good idea of the serious problems the English vowel system presents to the

[3] Please see the following word list for this symbol.

[4] For those unfamiliar with such symbols as ᴧ and ɔ, they are phonetic symbols specifying certain sounds. Here these sounds are provided by means of the word examples.

native speaker of Spanish. (You might listen again to some of the speakers and—based upon our discussion of vowel sounds—identify some of the problems you hear.

READING AND SPELLING

A native Spanish-speaking child whose first reading experience is in English (assuming, of course, that he or she has learned to *speak* English well before being asked to *read* it) will face a challenge similar to that faced by his native English-speaking classmate learning to read. However, a native Spanish-speaking student who learns to read in Spanish prior to English probably will encounter different problems in reading and spelling English. In learning to read Spanish, the child has learned to react to certain symbols (letters) in specified ways. When he sees the letter *a* in the word *para* (for), for example, he correctly associates it with the sound *a,* which he knows in such other words as *casa* (house). He learns to ignore the letter *h,* because in Spanish it represents no sound at all. For example, the word *hombre* (man) is pronounced *ombre,* as though the letter *h* were not there. These automatic habits, so carefully developed in learning to read Spanish probably will cause problems in learning to read English. The student may read the word *hair* as *air,* disregarding the letter *h,* much as he would in Spanish. He or she will expect a single vowel symbol such as the *a* in *cat, late,* and *father* to represent the same sound. It will be confusing that the same vowel sound can be represented by several different letters or letter combinations (e.g., the *u*-sound in *full, wood,* and *could*). Another matter of confusion will be that these same letters or letter combinations (*u, oo,* and *ou*) also may represent different sounds in other words (e.g., $\wedge$ in *cut,* uw in *food,* and $\supset$ in *cough*). Although there is no perfect one-to-one correspondence in Spanish between letters and the sounds they represent (e.g., both *c* and *qu* may represent the sound *k*) the relationship between letter and sound—especially vowels—is less variable than it is in English. The native Spanish-speaking student will expect the relatively unique correspondence between symbol and sound that is characteristic of Spanish to occur in English. The Spanish-speaking student who already has learned to read in Spanish thus will face two problems in learning to read English:

1. Learning to react differently to the letters he or she sees, i.e., learning to react to these letters as representing English, not Spanish sounds.
2. Learning that the consistency between symbol and sound expected in Spanish does not occur in English.

Consider the reading of Antonio, a 17-year-old student who first went to school in Mexico and learned to read in Spanish. Antonio had been in the United States a year and a half at the time of this recording. As you listen to this selection in English, note the effects of his having learned to read first in Spanish.

Last week a whole group of us guys wanted to go to the football game at Alamo Stadium. One of the guys said he could get his Dad's car that night so we wouldn't have to worry about getting there. It sounded like a good idea.

I went home to check with my Mom and Dad. They were in the kitchen when I got home, and they both looked like they were in a pretty good mood. So, I asked them if I could go to the game. They gave each other a funny look and walked into the other room.

I stayed alone in the kitchen thinking about what I could have done wrong this time. A month ago, I was grounded because I forgot to wash down the driveway and the floor of the garage with the hose after my Dad told me three times to do it. Another time I threw a baseball through the window of the garage. It was always something like that, just when I want to do something special. I tried to strain my ears to hear what they were saying, but it was useless because the door was closed tight.

I waited wondering what they could be saying about me. I even thought about my grades in school and wondered if my teacher told them something about my grades that I didn't know yet. Finally my Dad came out looking very stern. I was so nervous that I couldn't look my Dad in the face. I kept staring down at the tops of my shoes. If I knew what I was going to be accused of, I could be preparing a defense. But, I couldn't imagine what this was all about.

GRAMMAR

Although there are some aspects of English and Spanish grammar that are similar (e.g., the word order in such sentences as, "Estamos escribiendo la carta" and "We are writing the letter") there are many other aspects of Spanish and English that show marked contrast and often present serious problems to the second language learner. One such problem involves the suffixes employed in English to indicate that a noun is plural. When speaking of more than one *cat* English speakers add an -*s*. When speaking of more than one dog they add a -*z*. And when speaking of more than one church they add -$\land z$. Although Spanish nouns also are pluralized by adding a suffix to the noun—an -*s* to those words that end in a vowel and -*es* to words ending in consonants—the difference between the two languages is that the addition of two of the English plural suffixes often results in final consonant clusters. As we indicated above, such clusters never occur in Spanish. So the Spanish-speaking child often is heard to say, "two book" instead of "two books." This is not necessarily because he or she doesn't know how to make a plural but because the consonant sound combination *ks* at the end of the word is not within his or her repertoire of sounds and sound combinations.

Other grammatical suffixes that parallel the noun plural in English include the third-person singular, present-tense marker as in, "he run + *z*," "she sleep + *s*," and "he watch + $\wedge z$" and the noun possessive marker as in, "John + *z* book," Janet + *s* book," and "Rich + $\wedge z$ book." These suffixes result in the same consonant clusters described for the noun plural. Often, a Spanish-speaking child is diagnosed as not knowing given grammatical markers in English, and efforts are made to drill him on those markers. In reality, his problem may have more to do with the sound combinations that result from adding the grammatical markers to the ends of the words than with the grammatical markers themselves.

A similar problem involves the way English marks its past tense. A suffix again is added to the verb (e.g., jump + *t,* learn + *d,* and plant + $\wedge d$), and the resulting consonant clusters in the first two may present difficulties to the Spanish-speaking child. This is not necessarily because he or she doesn't know how to make the past tense but simply is not accustomed to discriminating and producing final consonant clusters. Those involved in teaching English to native Spanish-speaking children always must be alert to those sound combinations that inhibit the acquisition of these English grammatical suffixes.

Another difference between Spanish and English is that in Spanish the pronoun subject often may be omitted when it is clear to the speaker and listener who the subject is. Thus, if you were talking to someone about a mutual friend, John, you might say, "He's very thin" and in Spanish, "(El) es muy flaco." In English the subject pronoun *he* must be included. In Spanish, it may be included for emphasis, but it usually will be omitted if you and your friend already have established John as the topic of conversation. The option to omit the pronoun subject in Spanish often results in the Spanish-speaking child producing such English sentences as, "Is very pretty" or, "Is my friend." These, of course, are not grammatical English sentences.

In Spanish, adjectives may follow the noun they modify, and they agree with that noun in both number and gender. English adjectives typically precede the noun, and they do not change their form to agree with the noun they modify. Spanish-speaking children consequently might be heard to utter such combinations as "The shoes blues."

Possessive adjectives in English present another problem to the native, Spanish-speaking child. In Spanish, the possessive adjective (*mi, su, nuestro*) relates to the subject; but like all other adjectives, it agrees with the noun it modifies. In English, where adjectives do not agree with nouns, the possessive relates exclusively to the subject. When forming the possessive Spanish speakers must consider both the subject and the object possessive, whereas English speakers focus solely on the subject-possessor. For example, "We saw *our* sons" is "Vimos a *nuestros* hijos" in Spanish. "We saw *our* daughter" is "Vimos a *nuestra* hija." Note that in English the possessive *our* remains the same regardless of the object it modifies. In Spanish, on the other hand, the possessive *nuestros,* modifying a masculine plural noun, is changed to *nuestra* when modifying the feminine singular noun, *hija.* As a result of this difference in focus the Spanish speaker sometimes makes such statements as, "He loves her wife" instead of, "He loves his wife." The possessive adjective is considered as it relates to the object possessed—a feminine noun in this sentence—and "her" is used instead of "his" to agree with this feminine noun, *wife.*

Noun possessors, too, are indicated differently in Spanish and English. When the possessor is a noun rather than a pronoun Spanish employs the relator *de* to indicate the possessive relationship (e.g., "el libro de José" [literally, "the book of Joe"] for the English, "Joe's book"). Spanish speakers often follow this pattern when speaking English; and such utterances as, "The car of my father" and "the boyfriend of my sister" replace the English noun possessive constructions, "my father's car" and "my sister's boyfriend," in the Spanish speaker's English.

As mentioned previously, English and Spanish sentence patterns show many common features. In declarative sentences in both languages the subject typically precedes the verb, and if there is a noun object that object typically follows the verb. Thus, English, "John ate the oranges," and Spanish, "Juan comió las naranjas," are parallel sentences. On the other hand, if these sentences are changed to questions the Spanish and English patterns differ. In Spanish the word order may remain the same for the question, ¿Juan comió las naranjas?", or the verb may precede the subject as in, ¿Comió Juan las naranjas?" In English, however, the question corresponding to "John ate the oranges" requires the insertion of the tense-carrier *do* as in, "Did John eat the oranges?" The Spanish speaker generally finds this use of *do,* which also occurs in negative sentences, to be a problem. It is not uncommon to hear such sentences as, "Ate John the oranges?" and "John not ate the oranges."

The differences between the grammatical structures of English and Spanish presented here represent but a brief overview of some of the major points of contrast. The point is not to provide a complete inventory of contrasting grammatical aspects of the two languages but rather to point out that differences of this kind do exist throughout the grammatical systems in question. Thus, in teaching Spanish speakers English, problems resulting from these contrasting patterns and many others like them can be expected to occur. Consider now examples of the grammatical problems

just discussed that are encountered by Ramon, a 16-year-old native Spanish speaker, as he tells us the story of Cinderella.

Ramon: Once upon a time . . uh . . one little pretty girl lived with two sisters and their mother because their father are dead. Eh . . that princess, no, that girl, is doing all the work in the house because the old sisters, the other sisters, are very angry with he . . . with she . . . Mm . . and . . and one day the princess . . eh went at one party and invited all the girls to find a marriage with he, and the two sisters go, but Cinderella no, and she cried. But the . . . what is *hada*?

Who? Oh, the fairy . . . fairy godmother . . .

And the addy, aparecio . . .

Appeared.

. . . appeared and give a beautiful dress and a beautiful car, and Cinderella go to the party and dance all the night with the princess . . . prince, prince . . .

Prince.

. . . prince, but at twelve o'clock she must go, because the car and the dress is dis . . . disappeared . . .

Disappear?

. . . disappear. But . . eh . . the shoe . . . shoes forget it in the stair. The princess find in all the people . . eh . . eh . . who who's that shoes and when go to the Cinderella house and put on the two sisters and the Cinderella . . .

Cabe? . . . . fit?

Yeah . . . to fit the shoes and the dress and the . . . reappeared . . . reaparecio . . . reappeared?

Reappeared?

Yeh . . . reappeared and he and she married and lived very happy.

VOCABULARY

Because Spanish and English are historically related and because of many subsequent influences of one on the other, there are many words that look and sound alike and have the same meaning with only very minor differences in form. Such words are called *cognates.* For example:

Spanish	English	Spanish	English
crisis	crisis	teléfono	telephone
fotografía	photograph	segundo	second
planta	plant	especial	special
radio	radio	color	color
rodeo	rodeo	fantástico	fantastic

There are, however, other words that look alike but have quite different meanings. These words are called *false* or *deceptive cognates,* because they tend to lead the speaker of one language to assume that the word in the other language—which looks and sounds like the native language word—is a cognate. This occurs when, in fact, the two words do *not* have the same meaning. For example, the English verb *assist* appears similar to the Spanish verb *asistir.* But the similarity in form is deceptive, since it leads the Spanish speaker to assume that the English word functions the same as its Spanish counterpart when in fact it does not. For example, the Spanish speaker will say, "I am going to assist the class," based upon his Spanish, "Voy a asistir la clase," when in English the expected sentence is, "I am going to attend the class." The English word *parents* is similar to the Spanish word *parientes,* but in Spanish this word means relatives, not only parents. Accordingly, the Spanish-speaking child may say, "All my parents live in Puerto Rico." Another example involves the English word *fabric* and the Spanish word *fábrica* (factory), which look and sound alike but have quite different meanings. The Spanish-speaking child, assuming that the similar shape of these two words signifies a common meaning, is misled into responding to a question about his father's occupation with, "He is working in the fabric."

There are many such examples of false cognates in Spanish and English (notice, for example, how many pairs of words in the first sound list in this chapter are false cognates), and special attention must be paid to them.

REVERSE INFLUENCE

One last word involves the effects of the second language (in this case English) upon the first (Spanish). In Chapter 3 it was pointed out that languages that coexist in close proximity for a period of time affect each other. Spanish speakers in the United States are surrounded by English, and the influences of English upon their native Spanish are often considerable. For example, *alfombra* (carpet) often becomes *carpeta; frenos* (brakes) are *brecas; biblioteca* (library) is *librería;* and *periódico* (newspaper) becomes *papel.* And these influences from English are not limited to nouns. Spanish speakers may adapt English words to create such new Spanish verbs as *tichar* (from *teach*), *taipiar* (from *type*), *puchar* (from *push*), and *sainear* (from *sign*). Spanish speakers in an English-speaking environment also may incorporate multiple-word phrases from English into their Spanish. For example, they may say, "Tuvimos un buen tiempo," from the English, "We had a good time." Yet in Spanish *buen tiempo* refers to good weather, not to fun. One of the interesting results of this borrowing from English is that many of the false cognates and even some of the grammatical patterns discussed previously do not create problems for the native Spanish speaker whose dialect of Spanish already has been affected by English. A Spanish speaker in the United States may use *atender* instead of *asistir* as in, "Atendi la escuela," instead of "Asisti la escuela." The result, of course, is that this Spanish speaker has no difficulty with the English verb *attend* in such expressions as "attend school." It should be reemphasized here that these borrowings from English do not signify anything more than the inevitable results of two languages in contact affecting each other.

SUGGESTED ACTIVITIES

1. Compare the speech samples taken from Susan and Mary Beth. What features do you notice in Susan's speech that are not present in Mary Beth's?

2. If you are acquainted with people from a Spanish-speaking background, ask them to describe some differences between the way they speak Spanish and the way speakers they know from other Spanish-speaking countries or regions speak it. What are some of the differences they mention? If you speak Spanish, what regional differences do you notice in the Spanish of other speakers you know?

3. If you have contact with native Spanish-speaking children, make recordings of short speech samples of their English. Compare these samples with Susan's and Mary Beth's. Specify features in the speech samples you record that you believe result from interference from Spanish. Do the results of your study agree with the material presented in this chapter?

4. If you know Spanish and have contact with Spanish-speaking children, record speech samples in both English and Spanish and compare the two performances. In which language does each child appear to be dominant? How do you determine dominance? What pedagogical implications, if any, would you draw from this conclusion concerning language dominance?

5. If you are acquainted with native Spanish-speaking adults, ask them to tell you about the specific problems they encountered in learning English. Do their comments coincide with the information presented in this chapter?

6. In examining Luis's speech in this chapter, we discover in his Spanish many borrowed English words. English also has borrowed freely from other languages. Do you know the languages from which each of the following words was borrowed? If not, check your dictionary.

    A.   skunk
    B.   sputnik
    C.   algebra
    D.   picnic
    E.   guerrilla
    F.   buffalo
    G.   igloo
    H.   bonanza
    I.   ranch
    J.   snorkel
    K.   barbecue
    L.   cozy
    M.   canasta
    N.   tobacco
    O.   yogurt
    P.   patio

7. List all the sound substitutions that occur in the speech samples of Carlos and Gilberto. Are there similarities in the substitutions in the two samples? What aspect of the English sound system (consonant sounds, distribution of consonants, consonant clusters, vowel sounds) appears to give each speaker the greatest difficulty?

8. There are several native Spanish-speaking characters who appear regularly in television situation comedies. Are you familiar with any of them? If so, how do you know they represent native Spanish-speaking characters? When you have an opportunity to watch these programs record them if possible. Then make a list of those speech features that, in your opinion, reflect a Spanish influence on these characters' English. How authentic is the "accent" these characters use, in your opinion?

9. If you have contact with native Spanish-speaking adults, ask them to tell you about some of the difficulties they encountered in learning to read and spell in English.

Language Attitudes

6

THE GOOD LORD HELPS THOSE CHILDREN

The time was about 8:45 in a long evening. The scene was the cafeteria of a rural school where some 20 teachers had spent the last several hours studying videotapes of children who spoke the varied dialects found in that region of the United States. We had just finished a workshop on "Language Differences in Children," the goal of which had been to give the teachers some idea of why most linguists argue that dialect variations in children are more a case of language differences than deficits. As teachers most predictably do, the group had shown its enthusiasm for the project even through the coffee and cookie session that concluded the evening. But language attitudes run deep.

I know what you mean, how it's logical that children have different dialects. And I know that we should learn to be aware of them in developing our teaching materials. We have had a lot of talk about that here. Most of us agree that it's not really wrong if the child sounds like he is a Negro or Mexican. In fact, the good Lord has given extra blessings to these children. You should see those little Negro boys and girls on the playground—such energy and agility! And those Mexican children, they have a sense of colors matched by any no other group. I wish we had art classes for them.

117

The woman who made this comment was not a "bad" teacher. She had worked at the same school for 23 years, had paid her own way to the state university to take refresher courses nearly every summer. She had bought school materials for children whose parents could not afford them. This woman had devoted her life to the first-grade classroom. She had to do more in everyday, unglamorous work to accomplish the goals of her profession than most of us ever will be able to lay claim to. On the other hand, her whole view of the language of children was tied to stereotypes. She thought that if children looked and sounded a certain way, then you could expect them to act and learn a certain way. Perhaps her expectations were often accurate. But at the same time she probably was contributing to the fulfillment of her own prophecies in how she treated the children. Some people have called this the Pygmalion effect, drawing from the example of Eliza Doolittle and the well-known speech professor, Henry Higgins.

In this chapter, we will try to give you some idea of the nature of language attitudes, assuming that if we understand a little bit more about them they will create fewer problems. We will draw some examples from our own studies.

WHAT ARE LANGUAGE ATTITUDES?

Sonya is 12 and from California; she is having a conversation with an adult introduced to her as a teacher.

Sonya, what are some of the things that interest most 12-year-olds? You're a girl and you like to do certain things. What would they be?

Sonya: . . . cooking . . .

Cooking . . . good . . . Anything else?

Oh . . . (silence) . . . I like to babysit.

What's the best thing about babysitting?

(Silence) . . . I don't . . .

The money?

. . . no . . . (*very hushed tone*).

Oh boy—that'd be the best thing for me. What are your favorite families you babysit for?

. . . (Silence) . . . don't know . . .

Based on what Sonya had to say in this conversation, what do you think about her? Is she:

> Unsure or confident?
> Active or passive?
> Hesitant or eager?
> Intelligent or unintelligent?

Does she sound:

> Standard American or ethnic?
> Anglolike or non-Anglolike?
> Disadvantaged or advantaged?
> Happy or sad?

Is her family:

> High social status or low social status?
> Like yours or unlike yours?

The above types of impressions have been found consistently in how teachers talk about children when they hear brief language samples. Based on the sample, they would tend to judge Sonya as reticent and not particularly fluent; they might guess that she is an average or below-average student. But because there were no marks of nonstandardizations, Sonya would not be perceived as sounding "ethnic." Put another way, Sonya—for the little that she said—would be perceived as sounding "standard."

Compare Sonya's speech sample with a short segment from her brother, David (age seven).

> Okay, do you have any pets?
>
> *David:* Oh . . . I used to have a mouse, and we still have a rat.
>
> Well, what happened to your mouse?
>
> Oh, it ran away.
>
> Ran away? . . well, tell me about your rat.
>
> Oh, we found him in the sewer. No. We found him in the gutter . . . and we have different kind of gutters . . . and he was down. And our next door neighbor, Mr. Morrison, opened it up . . . . And opened it up and got the rat out.
>
> And gave it to you, uh?
>
> Yeh, and gave it to us.
>
> What are the kind of things you have to do for a rat?
>
> You have to clean his cage and feed him, and . . . and . . . give him a drink.

Teachers typically rate speech like David's as more "confident" and "eager" than samples like his sister's. At the same time, he would be rated as generally standard in dialect, as was his sister, Sonya. If we asked teachers to guess how well David does in school (and told them he was seven), they probably would feel that he was average or slightly above.

The main difference between David's and Sonya's speech samples is that David seems to take a more active role in responding to the interviewer's questions. There are fewer long, silent pauses in his speech. The interviewer needed to prompt David less to keep the conversation going, even including when David got mixed up in mentioning the gutter.

In a variety of studies, we have found that teachers almost always distinguish among children's speech samples in terms of two main types of attitudes. One is the quality of *confidence-eagerness* that distinguishes David's and Sonya's speech samples. The other is *ethnicity-nonstandardness,* which we will discuss shortly. It has been possible to measure these attitudes by placing adjective opposites at the ends of rating scales. Reconsider, for example, Sonya's and David's samples as you might rate each in terms of the following scale:

Most teachers would rate Sonya's sample as quite reticent, compared with David's, which was considerably more eager. Samples rated more "eager" than David's are those in which the child does most of the talking, even asking the interviewer a question or two. We have found in these studies that ratings of eagerness vs. reticence tend to reflect such speech characteristics as the following.

Eagerness	*Reticence*
Tends to answer questions fully.	Tends to need prompting to answer questions.
Sometimes asks questions.	Never asks questions.
Is usually fluent; few pauses.	Often has long, silent pauses.
Generally "speaks up," varies voice.	Hushed voice, monotone.

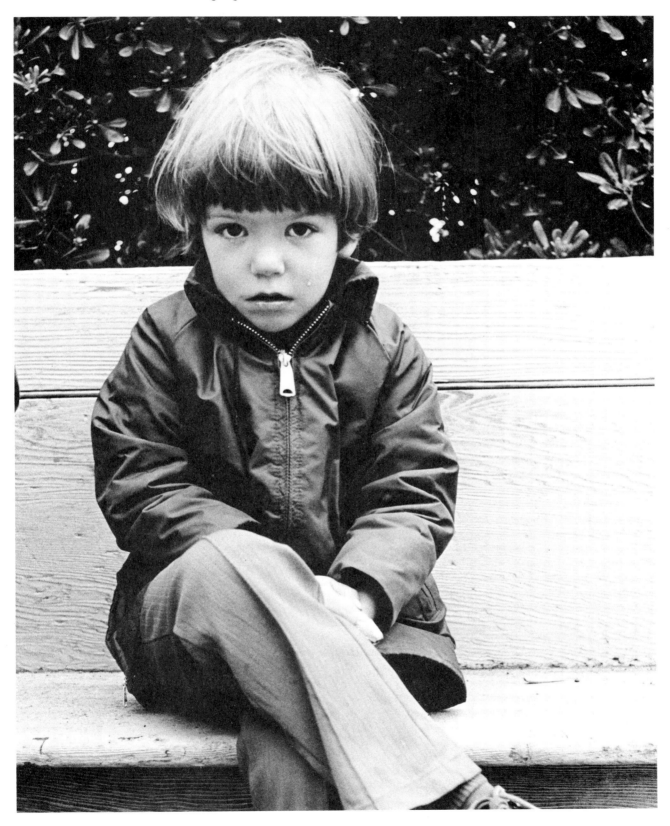

As we already have mentioned, listeners also react to the *ethnicity-nonstandardness* qualities of speech samples. Sonya and David were both generally perceived as *standard.* So if they were compared on a scale, the results probably would appear as follows.

```
                     David
                     |Sonya
                     |
                     |
Standard,            |                              Nonstandard,
nonethnic: ____ : ↓____ : ____ : ____ : ____ : ____ : ____ : ethnic
```

Consider attitudes both about eagerness and standardness as you read this sample from Kennedy, an eight-year-old black child. We have tried to capture a bit of the dialect in our spelling.

> And you play around your house, too, don't you?
> *Kennedy:* Yes, sir.
> What do you play around there mostly?
> Foo'ball . . . sometime we go to c fiel' an play foo'ball.
> Uh huh, uh huh.
> And sometime we play out d'ere in front of da hous.'
> (Uh huh, uh huh. And do you have brothers and sisters, Kennedy?)
> I have' five brother and two sister.
> You want to tell me something about them?
> One go to high school, she go to South Oak Cliff . . . and one go to _____; and one go to _____ over d'ere; and one go to Zumwalt; and two don't go.
> Two don't go?
> Huh uh.
> They're too little or something?
> Naw . . . they big!

Based on our experiences with language samples of these kinds; Kennedy would be rated as more eager than Sonya, about the same as David in terms of *confidence-eagerness.*

In terms of *ethnicity-nonstandardness,* Kennedy's rating probably would be as follows.

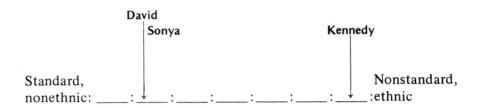

In a variety of studies we have found that merely the appearance of a non-standardization or two will prompt teacher-raters to consider a child's speech ethnic-sounding or nonstandard. Some of these characteristics follow.

Standard-nonethnic	*Nonstandard-ethnic*
Regular pronunciation of "th" as in "the."	Use of "d" for "th."
Regular pronunciation of "g" and "ing."	Omission of "g" or "ing" endings.
Use of regular "s" plural inflection.	Omission of "s" inflection as in "two cup."
Full pronunciation of consonant clusters.	Reduction of consonant cluster to one or no sound.
Verb-subject agreement.	Verb-subject disagreement as in "books is."

Additional characteristics are more direct features of a given dialect, such as those described in the chapters on black and Spanish-influenced English.

Language attitudes of *confidence-eagerness* and *ethnicity-nonstandard-ness* appear to be relatively separate from one another. That is, it is entirely feasible that a child who sounds ethnic also may sound confident (as did Kennedy); or a child may sound both ethnic and reticent. For an example of the latter, consider Gail. She is not as reticent as Sonya, but still not as eager as Kennedy or David.

All right. Are you pretty good at baseball?

Uh huh.

What . . . what . . . is tether ball about? What kind of game is that?

When you hi' da ball to nother person and you try to make it go all da way around da post uh . . . so dey won't catch it . . . hi' it hard nough.

(Uh huh . . . uh huh . . . and you, you like that?)

Uh huh.

You can really hit it and make it wrap itself around the post?

Yeah, yeah.

And you play baseball, too. You can hit pretty good?

Not too good.

You catch well?

Uh huh.

Good. Okay. Now what other games do you play, say, when you're home? What do you play? What sort of games?

We don' do ga . . . , too many games. We do cheers.

You do what?

Cheers.

Cheers? At home? Are you on the cheering squad or something like that?

Da bi' girls teach us.

Oh, I see. And what kind of cheers do they teach you? Can you say one for me?

Go lion . . .
Go lion . . . Figh'
We got spiri'
We got migh'
Go lion . . . figh'
Yea . . . lion.

Relative to the other children, Gail would be rated roughly as follows.

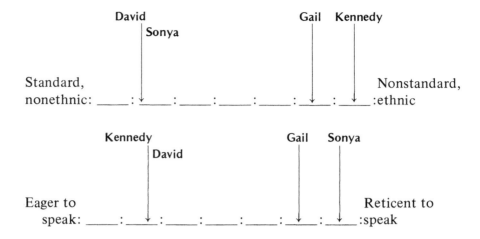

Again, Gail sounds more eager than Sonya, but less so than David or Kennedy. Her speech has ethnic characteristics, but it is not rated quite as nonstandard as Kennedy's is.

As mentioned earlier, these two, broad dimensions of language attitudes—*confidence-eagerness* and *ethnicity-nonstandardness*—are relatively independent of each other. Because of this, it sometimes is useful to see them in terms of the two-dimensional diagram shown in Figure 1. We purposely chose four language samples that would illustrate extremes in terms of the two main dimensions of language attitudes. David was rated standard-nonethnic and eager, as reflected in his lack of non-standardizations and his tendency to answer fully the questions put to him. Sonya was rated as standard, but by contrast she tended to respond passively to questions. Hence, she was rated as more reticent than was her brother. Kennedy was rated as eager as David was but also as sounding quite nonstandard. Gail's speech also was rated nonstandard. Because she tended to react passively on some questions, however, she was rated as more reticent than either David or Kennedy.

In a practical sense, Figure 1 illustrates at least two major types of attitudes toward children's speech as found in studies of teachers. We also have found that teachers tend to relate some of their academic expectations to language attitudes. For example, children rated as eager generally are expected to do slightly better overall in school than are children rated as reticent. Ratings of children in terms of ethnicity-nonstandardness are quite predictive of how well teachers feel a child will do in language arts subjects.

David would do well in school, including language arts subjects.

Kennedy would do well in school, but might have trouble in language arts.

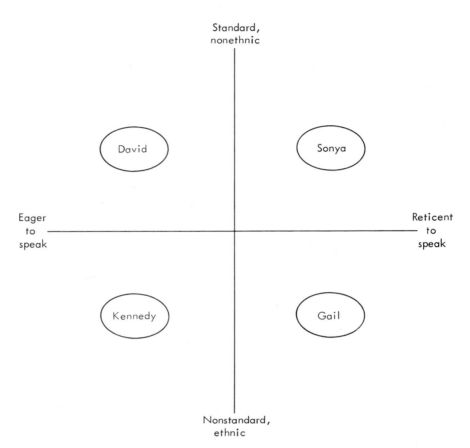

Figure 1. The two dimensions of language attitudes.

Sonya would be average or slightly below average in her subjects,
   but probably no more so in language arts than in any other
   subject.
Gail might be average or slightly below average in school and could
   be expected to have trouble in language arts subjects.

ARE LANGUAGE ATTITUDES ACCURATE?

In studies where we carefully have identified the linguistic characteristics of a speech sample, we found that groups of teachers generally are
accurate and consistent in differentiating the *samples* in terms of confidence-
eagerness and ethnicity-nonstandardness. We emphasize *samples*, because

the ratings are accurate according to what the teacher *hears,* not necessarily according to how the child *sounds* in his or her *usual* speaking habits. The question raised is: How good are the samples? In most of our studies we tried to replicate the situation of a child talking with a person introduced as a teacher. This creates a slight degree of formality and usually represents a standard English-speaking situation. Thus all we say about language attitude refers to speech under this particular type of situation, one that may be quite different from a child's performance, say, on the playground.

For the most part, however, we are more interested in what studies have revealed about teachers than about the details of children's speech. For example, some teachers can be "fooled" into hearing nonstandard speech if the video image of a black child is paired with a standard English sound track. In this study we took a speech sample that was carefully analyzed to indicate the lack of nonstandardizations and combined it with the videotape of a black child or one of a Mexican-American child. Thus, the children appeared to be speaking in a televised representation. Some teachers apparently responded so directly to the video image that they rated the speech as ethnic-sounding. It may be that some teachers—albeit a small minority—are so prone to hearing a particular type of speech from a child of a given race that they hardly can hear otherwise. This raises obvious problems for the many black and Mexican-American children who can speak standard English as the occasion warrants it.

Another insight into teacher's attitudes was provided by our study of how much an individual teacher thought a child's speech might vary. Given a speech sample, the teacher was asked to mark (say, with a check) how they might expect that child to sound at different times and also to mark (with a "0") how they *never* expected them to sound. (A blank means "undecided.") Thus a rating might look like the following.

Eager to   Reticent to
  speak: _0_ : _0_ : _0_ : ____ : _√_ : _√_ : _√_ :speak

In rating the same children, some teachers varied markedly in how much latitude they expected in a child's speech. Remember that Sonya was rated as reticent. Now consider the difference in the following two teachers' ratings of Sonya's speech latitude.

Teacher I

Eager to   Reticent to
  speak: _0_ : _0_ : _0_ : _0_ : _0_ : _√_ : _√_ :speak

Teacher II

Eager to   Reticent to
speak: __0__ : _____ : _____ : _√_ : _√_ : _√_ : _√_ :speak

Teacher I would never expect to hear Sonya sound much different than in the sample. In contrast, Teacher II would expect Sonya to sound more eager at times. Teacher II is less inclined to believe that Sonya would *never* sound as eager as the halfway point on the scale (remember that blank means "undecided"). Such measures have given us evidence that some teachers simply are more closed-minded than others in terms of the degree to which they think a child might sound different. What happens, then, in real life when a child does vary his or her speech? Does such a teacher recognize it?

IS THERE ANYTHING WRONG WITH LANGUAGE ATTITUDES?

There is nothing *inherently* wrong with language attitudes. They are part of the processes of perception, learning, and expectations. We generalize from our experiences in trying to predict how another human will act, what will happen next, and so on. The kinds of attitude measures discussed previously generally are accurate for the given sample, and having expectations of a child's academic capabilities may be somewhat better for us than no expectations at all. On the other hand, studies of linguistic attitudes have revealed that some teachers have a relatively narrow view of what a child who speaks a certain way is capable of accomplishing. That is, a teacher may be relatively insensitive to the individual differences found within a group of children of a particular type. His or her perceptions of certain groups of children may be inflexibly *stereotyped.* Although sociologists and psychologists have a variety of definitions for stereotypes, what we mean is that a teacher sometimes will consider a child *categorically* as one type or another without being particularly sensitive to the details of his or her language performance.

The main point here is that some of our language attitudes seem highly tied to expectations that may not be directly influenced by the detailed characteristics of the child doing the speaking. That is, attitudes may be very much influenced by whether we perceive the child as black, white, low-class, middle-class, rural, urban, and so on. In the study involving combinations of different children and speech samples, the visual image of the child presumably prompted stereotypes that affected speech ratings.

Due to segregated school systems and lack of opportunity in the United States, language and academic stereotypes might have some degree of accuracy. But such stereotypes may prevent a teacher from observing change in a given child—particularly in a minority group child. This is when there is something wrong with language attitudes. There are very serious problems in negative attitudes when they cause us to have fixed expectations about children, when these stereotypes affect our very capability of *seeing* differences or changes in the children. This is the negative situation wherein we influence the children to fulfill our own prophecies about them.

IS THERE ANYTHING THAT WE SHOULD TRY TO CHANGE?

Certainly there are changes to be made in language attitudes. But to be practical, there are at least two things we can do something about now.

1. Avoid narrow stereotypes that prevent us from seeing variation (or change) in certain children.
2. Constantly reassess the associations we make between speech characteristics and academic expectations.

The admonition here is that language attitudes should not become too much of an inhibiting factor when predicting a child's academic potential. It is important to understand that many language cues that prompt attitudes—such as the simple "d" for "th" substitution—are not usually barriers to communication. They are insignificant to a linguist, because they represent nothing more than superficial variations in the expressed form of language. It often is said that such features are of more social than linguistic significance. That is, they do more to prompt social attitudes in the listener than they do to affect the basic content of the message being communicated. Obviously, the implication for teachers is to sort out these kinds of markers and not let them bias attitudes—and hence, the entire educational expectations held of a child. To put the problem more practically, some of the associations between linguistic attitudes and academic expectations may be so arbitrary as to merit avoidance or constant reassessment. We are quite capable of changing these associations directly in our own minds and of alleviating at least some of the problems.

In conclusion, it is important to emphasize that we are *not* trying to include everything that might be said on the topic of language and children. What we have done is to concentrate on the few, simple points we have made. For one thing, language attitudes are a volatile social topic. How people feel about each other's language is a very direct example of how they

feel about one another. To presume that teachers can extricate themselves from the whole social context within they were reared and which the school may unfortunately have demanded of them is unreasonable. None of us can easily remove ourselves from our social context; instead, we must work within it and with an awareness of it.

To concentrate on the child, we have not made any major point about what the term "standard" connotes. Most precisely, it is a term in linguistics literature that refers to a dialect of American English spoken probably most consistently by people in certain parts of the Midwest. Whether *standard* means *preferred* is quite another issue—one settled more on the grounds of social attitudes than linguistic ones.

There is, of course, the question of whether children who speak a dialect other than standard should be the target of educational programs of change. Linguistically speaking there is a variety of dialects of English, and standard is only one of them. The question of whether a child who speaks a nonstandard dialect should try to change is not one that can be debated well in this book. It may be more a social question than a linguistic one. Humans are quite capable of speaking multiple dialects. Idealistically, there should be nothing considered "wrong" with anybody's dialect, so long as it is not a barrier to intelligibility. In fact, research indicates that American dialects offer little barrier to intelligibility (except when attitudes cause interference).

We have emphasized that language attitudes are a very vital part of our everyday dealings, particularly with classroom children. Here are some summary generalizations:

There is evidence of global types of language attitudes toward the apparent confidence-eagerness and ethnicity-nonstandardness of a child's speech.

Confidence-eagerness seems tied to lack of hesitancy in speech, as well as to carrying the conversational ball.

Ethnicity-nonstandardness tends to reflect particular linguistic (dialect) characteristics of utterances.

Attitudes concerning confidence-eagerness seem tied somewhat to an overall degree of academic expectations; whereas attitudes about ethnicity-nonstandardness seem tied particularly to academic expectations in the language arts areas.

We can avoid some of the problems of linguistic attitudes by increasing our capability of sensing differences and changes in children's speech.

We can further avoid biased academic expectations by carefully reconsidering the kinds of associations we make between language characteristics and academic predictions.

SUGGESTED ACTIVITIES

1. Play recordings of the four children in this chapter—David, Sonya, Gail, and Kennedy—for a friend, a class you are teaching, or for anyone interested in language. Ask them to jot down a few words about what they think each child is like. Do the descriptions have some characteristics in common with the scale markings we summarized?

2. Make up some simple scales from the 10 questions about Sonya on page 119. Here's a suggested format:

Unsure ____ : ____ : ____ : ____ : ____ : ____ : ____ Confident

Eager ____ : ____ : ____ : ____ : ____ : ____ : ____ Hesitant

Etc.

Put the 10 scales on one master sheet; then make duplicates. Ask people to listen to the recordings and to put a check mark somewhere between each pair of adjectives to indicate their rating of the speaker. Have them fill out one sheet of scales for each speaker. Do the results generally agree with our discussion? Use the results as a basis for a discussion of linguistic attitudes.

3. Use the same sets of scales for ratings of children drawn from any group of interest to you. See if you obtain the same kinds of rating differences as we used to distinguish the children discussed in this chapter.

4. Use the same sets of scales, but this time have listeners put multiple check marks on each scale to indicate the degree to which they might *expect* differences in how that child might sound. Ask them to put in "0" for differences they would *not* expect. Use your own language samples, or compare David and Gail on our recording. What differences do you find in the speakers? What differences do you find among listeners?

5. After studying this chapter, make some language samples of yourself in which you try to vary your speech to sound eager or hesitant, ethnic or nonethnic. Can you do it? If so, try to obtain some scale ratings to see if you succeeded.

READINGS AND REFERENCES

ABRAHAMS, ROGER, and TROIKE, RUDOLPH C. (eds.) *Language and Cultural Diversity in American Education.* (Englewood Cliffs, New Jersey: Prentice-Hall, Inc., 1972).

BROWN, ROGER. *A First Language.* (Cambridge, Massachusetts: Harvard University Press, 1973).

BURLING, ROBBINS. *English in Black and White.* (New York: Holt, Rinehart and Winston, 1972).

DALE, PHILIP. *Language Development: Form and Function.* (New York: Dryden, 1972).

DE STEFANO, JOHANNA S. (ed.) *Language Culture and Society: A Profile of Black English.* (Worthington, Ohio: Charles A. Jones, 1973).

GUMPERZ, JOHN. "The Speech Community," in *International Encyclopedia of the Social Sciences.* (New York: Macmillan, 1968) pp. 381-86.

HOPPER, ROBERT, and NAREMORE, RITA C. *Children's Speech: A Practical Introduction to Communication Development.* (New York: Harper & Row, 1973).

LENNEBERG, ERIC. *Biological Foundations of Language.* (New York: John Wiley, 1966).

MALMSTROM, JEAN, and ASHLEY, ANNABEL. *Dialects U.S.A.* (Champaign, Illinois: National Council of Teachers of English, 1963).

STOCKWELL, ROBERT P., and BOWEN, J. DONALD. *The Sounds of English and Spanish.* (Chicago, Illinois: University of Chicago Press, 1965).

STOCKWELL, ROBERT P., BOWEN, J. DONALD, and MARTIN, JOHN W. *The Grammatical Structures of English and Spanish.* (Chicago, Illinois: University of Chicago Press, 1965).

WILLIAMS, FREDERICK. (ed.) *Language and Poverty: Perspectives on a Theme.* (New York: Academic Press, 1970; formerly Markham and Rand McNally).

WILLIAMS, FREDERICK. *Language and Speech.* (Englewood Cliffs, New Jersey: Prentice-Hall, Inc., 1972)

WILLIAMS, FREDERICK. *Explorations of the Linguistic Attitudes of Teachers.* (Rowley, Massachusetts: Newbury House, in press).

WOLFRAM, WALT and FASOLD, RALPH W. *The Study of Social Dialects in American English.* (Englewood Cliffs, New Jersey: Prentice-Hall, Inc., 1974).

Index